RACISM

RACISM

Stories on fear, hate & bigotry

Edited by Winnie Dunn, Stephen Pham & Phoebe Grainer

First published in 2021
by Sweatshop Literacy Movement Inc.
I.C.E. (Information & Cultural Exchange)
8 Victoria Road, Parramatta NSW 2150, Australia
www.sweatshop.ws

Printed and bound by McPherson's Printing Group
Cataloguing-in-Publication data is available from
the National Library of Australia

ISBN 978-0-9924886-6-6 (paperback)

Design and typesetting by Elaine Lim
and Henry Lo 2021

PACKER FAMILY
FOUNDATION

ACKNOWLEDGEMENTS

This anthology has been developed by Sweatshop: Western Sydney Literacy Movement in partnership with Campbelltown City Library as part of the Campbelltown Youth Literacy Initiative for Diverse Writers. Proudly supported by the Crown Resorts Foundation and Packer Family Foundation.

Sweatshop is supported by I.C.E. (Information & Cultural Exchange), the Australian Government through the Australia Council, its arts funding and advisory body, Diversity Arts Australia and Red Room Poetry.

PRODUCTION TEAM

EDITORS: Winnie Dunn, Stephen Pham & Phoebe Grainer

ADVISORY EDITORS: Michael Mohammed Ahmad & Sarah Ayoub

COMMISSIONING EDITOR: Sydnye Allen

SUB-EDITORS: Mark Mariano & Divya Venkataraman

DESIGN & TYPESETTING: Elaine Lim & Henry Lo

COVER ARTIST: Jonathan Tumbel

COVER MODEL: Akwasi Appiah

SCHOOL WORKSHOP FACILITATORS: Winnie Dunn, Sydnye Allen, Michael Mohammed Ahmad, Keanah Scholes, Phoebe Grainer & Stephen Pham

SPECIAL THANKS: Paula Pfoeffer, Lina Kastoumis, Francisco Lopez, Kate Clarkson, Rosemary Ferris, Yvette King, Anne Loxley & Lena Nahlous

TABLE OF CONTENTS

MICRO AGGRESSIVE FICTION

INTRODUCTION

Winnie Dunn, Stephen Pham & Phoebe Grainer

We begin by acknowledging the Traditional Custodians of the land on which each writer wrote these stories. We pay our respect to their Elders past, present and emerging. These stories are now part of the big story that is in the earth that we live, sleep and eat off. Aboriginal Land. Bama Butcheree. Land of the Black Nations of this big island. We would like to acknowledge that the stories in this collection are inherently connected to the realities that we live each and every single day of our lives. Aboriginal sovereignty has never been ceded. These are Aboriginal lands, Aboriginal rivers, Aboriginal seas and Aboriginal oceans. Always was. Always will be.

—

Australia is racist. Since 1991, at least four hundred and seventy-four Indigenous people have been murdered in custody. In 2019, fifty-one Muslims peacefully conducting their Friday prayers were gunned down at Al Noor Mosque and Linwood Islamic Centre in Christchurch by an Australian-born White supremacist. In 2020, the Brereton Report recorded that Australian special forces had committed at least thirty-nine unlawful killings of Afghan civilians.

In the wake of COVID-19, more than one thousand Asian-Australians reported incidents of racial discrimination. And to date, almost two thousand refugees are held and denied basic human rights in detention facilities across the country and in off-shore detention; over ten Pacific seasonal workers have died on Australian farmlands due to squalid living conditions, mistreatment and insufficient medical assistance; and in the suburbs of North Melbourne and Flemington, African-Australians are two-and-a-half times more likely to be stopped by police than any other group.

In spite of these figures, many Australians still deny that racism is a problem in this country. In 2005, over five thousand White Australians chanted 'Fuck off Lebs' on the shores of Cronulla, physically assaulting anyone they recognised as 'Middle Eastern'. Shortly after the infamous Cronulla Riots, then-Prime Minister John Howard proclaimed, 'I do not accept that there is underlying racism in this country. I have always taken a more optimistic view of the character of the Australian people. I do not believe Australians are racist.' More recently, Prime Minister Scott Morrison claimed that the Black Lives Matter movement, an internationally renowned and respected protest against state-sanctioned violence inflicted on Black communities, should not be 'imported' to Australia. And, just eleven days into 2021, NSW Premier Gladys Berejiklian said in a press conference, 'I don't believe that we have an inherent problem with racism. I don't.'

We created this book to set the record straight.

Racism: Stories on Fear, Hate & Bigotry is an anthology for Australians, all Australians, who require an honest reflection of the racism that is present and prevalent in the lives of so many of our citizens. Through these stories, we seek to provide a personal and intimate record from First Nations people and people of colour, across all ages, that demonstrates the pain, despair, confusion, complexity and rejection that comes with being the 'other'.

Since 2013, Sweatshop Literacy Movement has been facilitating three distinct literary collectives: the Western Sydney Writers Group, the Sweatshop Women Collective, and most recently, the Black Lives Workshops. Now, at last, we have brought together every writer from every collective in our entire organisation for this one single anthology.

From the outset of the project, we knew that we wanted to create a book that was raw, honest, provocative and compelling. This began with a title that had no literary pretentions. *Racism: Stories on Fear, Hate & Bigotry* is not abstract, figurative, ironic or satirical. It is a title that lets you know, before you open to the very first page, that we are here to have a serious conversation with Australia about race.

To complement the title, we equally recognised that the cover image needed to speak to this moment in time, representing the struggle, as well as the strength, courage and beauty, that comes with being a person of colour in the year 2021. The image for our cover was taken by Indonesian-Australian photographer, Jonathan Tumbel, and features Ghanaian-Australian model, Akwasi Appiah. Jonathan and Akwasi drew inspiration for the image from the anthology's opening story, 'Invasions', which was written by African-American writer, Tyree Barnette. Tyree's contribution to this publication explores the diversity of the Black diaspora – held together by the waters of Santo, Vanuatu.

Alongside Tyree, the writers of Sweatshop, both new and familiar, dissect racism in all its forms. For Sara Saleh, racism is war, displacement and the disconnection from our motherlands. For Sydnye Allen, racism is passive-aggressive, predictable and ever-present. For Mark Mariano, racism is self-hatred. For Rizcel Gagawanan, racism is performance. For Daniel Nour, racism is shame. For Janette Chen, racism is lyrical. Natalia Figueroa Barroso calls racism colonisation. Christine Shamista calls it a one-sided dialogue and Meyrnah Khodr calls it Islamophobia. Guido Melo and Heikmah Napadow show us that racism begins in childhood and Adam Phillip Anderson demonstrates how it follows us into adulthood. In the stories by Ferdous Bahar, Monikka Eliah and Ting Huang, racism is stereotyping, pre-judging and discriminating. In Shirley Le's piece, racism is divided across socio-economic lines as much as it is based on the colour of one's skin. For Amani Haydar, racism is subtle and for Pamela Asare, racism is invisible. Wiradjuri writer, Max Edwards, identifies racism as White supremacy, violent colonisation, the ongoing oppression of First Nations people; and Arab-Australian author, Sarah Ayoub, who takes us home with her breathtaking conclusion, identifies racism as 'the Australian story'.

Racism: Stories on Fear, Hate & Bigotry is also graced with the voices of the next generation of Sweatshop Writers. Our team had the honour of working with First Nations, migrant and refugee students from Lurnea IEC and Leumeah High School. Over a period of six months, these inspiring young people unpacked the intersections between race and teenagehood in modern-day Australia: what it means to be 'Aboriginal', what it means to be 'Aussie', and what it means to be 'ethnic'. They also explored White privilege, colourism, White male violence, Trumpism and the 2020 US elections. Several of these pieces are interspersed throughout the anthology, while others are featured in a special collection of nanotales called 'Micro Aggressive Fiction'. Through their work, these students demonstrate that it is never too early to learn about racism, talk about racism, write about racism, and prepare ourselves for a world that is too often built on fear, hate and bigotry.

As the editors of this anthology, we represent Aboriginal, Pasifika and Asian communities. Our assistant editors represent Arab-Muslim, Arab-Maronite and African-American identities. The writers of this book come from Indigenous, Palestinian, Māori, Tongan, Sāmoan, Assyrian, Lebanese, Bengali, Somali, Vietnamese, Chinese, Ghanaian, African-American, Iraqi, Sri Lankan, Afro-Brazilian, Uruguayan, Indian, Iranian, Nepali, Indonesian, Greek, Afghan, Filipinx and Egyptian backgrounds. The production team, including the designers and sub-editors, herald from Cambodian, Chinese, Indian and Filipinx communities. As a collective, we represent the voice of three generations of Australians who have experienced racism. In this book, we share these experiences with you. No longer can anyone deny that racism exists.

INVASIONS

Tyree Barnette

'Abbata bateek?'

I shook my head, smiling to hide my embarrassment. 'No, sorry! English only.' The bearded man blinked a few times, his face frozen in a smile. His hairy wiry arms, the colour of cedar, fell by his side. Then he laughed lightly and pointed to a canoe stretched along the shallow shore. I nodded.

My wife Tracina and I biked down to the ribbon of river on one of Santo's two-lane roads. Our destination was the famed Riri Blue Hole, one of the massive basins of freshwater on the island of Santo in Vanuatu.

We rode past the site on electric bikes initially expecting some tacky display, like those ridiculous roadside attractions in our home country of the USA. They beckon you to marvel at the largest sculpture of a peach in the land or to Instagram yourself beside a giant statue of Donald Trump wearing a bikini. Vanuatu, on the other hand, had few street markers. Locations were relative inside the South Pacific island nation and often defined by foreign infrastructure. Someone could live at Pepsi; meaning the closest landmark to their house was a billboard advertising the American soft drink.

Vanuatu would be my first encounter with Pacific members of the African diaspora on their own soil. I swapped curious looks, smiles and whispers with the locals. We were two sides of a mirror. I noticed the features of their Blackness were different to my American variety: rounded craniums framed flattened foreheads that stood over large, filled nostrils; marble-shaped eyes poked forward and fronted an oval head – these uniform facial attributes masked with syrup, cinnamon and umber.

At the stream, Beard Man's cedar hue matched the colour of the canoe that he slithered offshore. Drops of water jewelled his thick hair in the sun. The holes in his grey singlet inhaled a breeze and tossed around his thin muscled frame like a sail. His skinny legs went just past knee-deep in the water before he beckoned us over as he held the canoe still.

I waded in, picked up my leg and fished it around trying to get a foothold in the rocking boat. Around me, Santo's water churned like the flame of a blow torch. Once secure, I lurched forward.

Tracina was even less graceful. Beard Man chuckled, ushering her on with long wavy fingers while keeping the boat as tame as he could, his yellowed teeth a contrast to his charcoal beard. I gave her a hand and we floated along, the canoe's oars caressing the silky fire in rhythm. Beard Man did his best to point out native creatures around us between strokes. He shot a bony finger towards a glowing fish or to small neon green frogs gliding beneath the blaze.

'I'm sorry, what are you pointing to?' I enquired when I wasn't sure.

Beard Man gazed his marbles at me. Then he flexed his finger, pointing more demonstratively with excitement and raising his thick eyebrows into his flat forehead. I nodded and smiled broadly, pretending like I'd seen it. Around us, the emerald crowns of trees emblazoned by the sun bent and stroked the water below for a drink – some lost limbs for their effort, their mahogany flesh floating in the fire or unravelling on land back into Santo. Along the shore, dilapidated wooden huts stood bowlegged with stained and ragged cloth curtains in their windows. The silky inferno inched closer to toppling them.

A tropical bird the colour of Skittles darted in for a drink. I followed its blurred flight back up to a gnarled tree with a huge tumour of hideous wood. Suddenly, I jumped off the bench, irritating the tame boat and knocking an oar out of Beard Man's hand. 'Yoooo, the fuck is that?' I shrieked. The tumour grew claws and scurried up the tree with loud taps. All my organs shrunk to half their size and plummeted into the bottom of my stomach. The creature was the spawn of a tarantula and a tortoise. It had a hairy exterior covered in a dusty grey, the complexion of a mummified body. The crab spider moved like something out of *Arachnophobia*; one clawed leg in front of another, finding bits of soot-coloured bark to pull itself up on.

I imagined those legs carrying its heavy girth up my body. I would lay as petrified as Jeff Daniels' character near the end of the film when the tarantula slinked over his dark slacks. The claws would snap open my shins and the crab spider would engorge itself onto my scarlet marrow with its saliva-covered mouth pieces. The enormous shell would pin me down as I writhed in pain. The pincers would rip open my mouth and the crab would deposit milk-coloured eggs down my throat. I wouldn't be able to breathe feeling its eggs in my stomach stretching my organs. New crab spiders would hatch, eat through my torso and pour out of me, adorned in my organs. Beard Man's laughter snapped me back into the boat. The skin around his marbles seemed to peel further back as his beard parted.

Tracina dropped her lip and twitched her eyebrows. 'Really? You're scared of a coconut crab?' she spat as my trembling settled. It was the same reaction I got a few years ago on my birthday: a frigid snowy December in North Carolina. I was on my way back from having a beer and dinner with friends when my tyres skated over a patch of ice less than a mile from home. My shimmering grey Camry went sledding off the road so swiftly that I had to dodge a light pole. I sat there in my hoodie in near-death sweat and farts until Tracina arrived in her forest green Nissan. Rolling down her window with a glowing peanut butter hue and glistening locked hair across her shoulder, she remarked, 'Really? You can't drive in the snow?'

Beard Man might have picked out a few English words, or maybe it was from Tracina's tone, but a second convulsion of laughter hit him. He calmed down enough to grab his oar from the swirling magma and continued paddling.

'Fucking hellraiser crab!' I caught my breath and took my seat again. Ahead, one of Santo's watery wombs revealed itself in a deep lake. Mist oozed off the unspoiled surface. The scene was so perfect it looked like a screensaver.

We neared a short uneven dock where a couple of half-dressed locals secured our canoe. They spoke to Beard Man in one of Santo's dialects. One of them wore a baseball cap that lost its scarlet colour three shades ago. He was topless; a large, smooth gut tumbling over the waistband of his black gym shorts. When he spoke, so did his deep belly button. 'Elcum brotha and seesta to the Riri Blue Ole!' The hat shaded his chestnut face but I could still make out the ni-Vanuatu Black of flattened forehead and nose. Bits of moustache and stubble crowded his mouth and chin. 'One thousand vatu,' he requested.

I fished out my wallet and handed over the fee. The Gut counted a few bright pieces of paper and gave some to Beard Man. This was a local custom I read about on some travel blogs before arriving: you pay a small fee to the local landowners to enjoy whatever attractions exist on their private property. The fees cover the cost of maintaining the site itself and supporting the local community.

But Beard Man's face turned into a frown and he growled, motioning with his hands at the river. The Gut protested a bit, taking off his hat while gesturing. Their main language within the mass of spoken dialects on the island was Pidgin, a mix of English and local tongues. I could pick out 'canoe', 'long' and 'water' from their exchange.

They settled their argument with The Gut giving Beard Man more money. Beard Man then rolled his marbles over to me. He stiffened his limbs, veins protruding out of his cedar flesh; stretched his eyelids as far back as they could go, and emitted short deep yelps. For a moment, I thought he was having a seizure. Then he shot a finger up in the air and longer sustained yells tumbled out of his beard. For final effect, he stuck a water bottle into his pocket with his other hand, letting the liquid spill into his pants and darken the crotch of his grey shorts as if he'd pissed himself. Laughter tumbled out of The Gut, quaking his stomach. Tracina snickered beside me with a hand to her mouth.

'Oh, it's funny... until it lays eggs in you,' I remarked, shedding my clothing for the water.

'No worries mah brudda,' The Gut reassured me. 'Yuh too skinny for coconut crab!'

I leapt forward, my body shattering the sapphire surface. Underwater, Santo explored my new Blackness. It inspected my hair texture, stretching and dissolving away the coconut and almond oils running through my short brown curls, which were not nearly as thick as the ni-Vanuatu's. My skin soaked in waterproof sunscreen was familiar enough; somewhere between walnut and umber. But my short thin beard, shallow cheekbones and tall forehead were all strange features on the same face for Santo.

Suddenly, a child appeared behind a wall of bubbles. She wore a crest of fire: bright orange hair shooting out in all directions. She waved and we surfaced together. I saw more locals gathering by the water. Their molten blonde hair crashed onto foreheads of penny, peanut and pecan skin with matching flattened noses and foreheads, marble eyes and oval-shaped skulls. They marched out of the thicket wearing floral patterned skirts, afros, cornrows and basketball shorts. A few more kids flung themselves off a rope swing hanging by the pier, their lava hair joining the inferno below.

As the bodies splashed in one after the other, I heard a sudden rustling and a few muffled crashes – something heavy had hit Santo's bushy green curls. I looked around and others seemed to hear it too. Above, several Skittles fled from the emerald crowns of trees. Through the brush, I made out the snarling metallic grill of a pickup truck.

Four people jumped out like frantic lobsters before the boil, doors slamming, and headed towards the water. They chatted loudly in a European language; not the Romantic languages they swooned to us in grade school like Spanish or French. It was harsher, split the air.

'Kava vodka paroosky me ah slava.'

'Ah, marook navel nova Coca Cola!'

The Gut grinned eagerly, welcoming the newcomers by tucking his stomach into his shorts. The first man out of the pickup, who had a torso shaped like a beer fridge, waved him off with a tatted arm and stomped onto the pier. He wore a singlet with the words 'Phuket' emblazoned across it in fluorescent type. A white beach towel flapped from his rouge shoulders and joined the frayed ends of his cut-off jean shorts. Sandals held his fat feet in place, the fleshy bits squeezed out of the shoes' material like cooked meat bound in twine. There were two other men, skinnier with shades, baseball caps and zinc oxide caked down their noses and splashed across their cheeks. One of them clutched a box of assorted beers under a sinewy arm.

Behind the three men was the fourth person, a thin woman with a bright floral bikini over her pale skin. Her swimsuit matched the flames swirling in the water. Ghostly blonde hair was tied back on her head. In one hand, she carried a large straw hat that she used to swat away ni-Vanuatu children from her path. They responded by mocking her awkward tiptoeing stroll to the water over ant hills and rocks – sticking their arms out pretending to swat at each other's heads, their wet matted hair resembling old burlap bags.

The Europeans all took a moment to survey the ethereal scene around them while the children looked on curiously. Leaning on the edge of the dock, The Gut, still smiling, greeted them and asked for the fee. Ignoring him, one of the skinnier men pulled out a camera and started taking photos of five ni-Vanuatu children observing nearby. The man removed his shades, crossed his cobalt blue eyes and touched his pointy nose with his tongue, hoping to get a smile from them. The kids stared back blankly as Beard Man stepped in between them and the camera. He gave Skinny Camera Man an angry glare before hustling the kids into a short wooden hut nearby.

Tracina, floating beside me, furrowed her brow. 'Did he just fucking do that… like those babies are props?'

'Fee? Why fee? It's open to public. We drove here. No gates,' Tatted Man complained, his loud slow speech thick with rolling Rs. There was genuine surprise in his tone, punctuated by the rise of his pitch.

Pale Woman stirred a manicured crimson toe in the water as The Gut insisted, 'This is our land. We mek a living here. You have to pay.' His pronunciation improved the more agitated he became, the garbled syllables floating on the base of his voice separating from one another.

The ni-Vanuatu's ability to command who accessed their land and request payment from visitors was not common. The world had already clawed its way in. Our hosts, a retired White Australian couple from Brisbane, told us about fellow Aussies owning dozens of seaside properties in Luganville, the island's capital. They said that Japan claimed Santo's bounty of grass-fed cattle for imported beef and that the richest person on Santo was a Chinese man whose businesses included the grocery store we shopped at, an adjoining tax office and a laundromat. According to a local driver that our hosts connected us with, China had built Santo's new airport, the one we'd flown into. They also built an agricultural university, which we passed on the way to our accommodation. All this infrastructure and 'goodwill' paved the way for access and immigration to the island.

The Gut's patience wore thin, the top of his bulge peeking out over his waistband. He demonstrated just how much of the land surrounding the blue hole belonged to the local village – one arm shooting out through the shimmering jade curtain to a road out of view and the other pointing along the water's edge.

'Therrre wuss no sign, nothing!' Tatted Man shouted back in a raised, nasally retort. 'How yuh prove these your lands?'

'Schnitzel vittle high lem shire!' Pale Woman added.

'It's only a few dollars!' I blurted at them from the water nearby. The whole group twisted sharply toward Tracina and me, as if seeing us for the first time. Then Pale Woman turned back to Beard Man, scoffed at him and popped on her straw hat, inviting Skinny Camera Man to take pictures of her by the water.

The exchange splashed memories into my face of the blatant disrespect and disregard hurled at Black spaces back in the United States. I recalled some disagreements between the residents of a gentrified neighbourhood in Washington, D.C. and Howard University, a prestigious, historically Black institution. African-Americans started well over a hundred HBCUs (Historically Black Colleges and Universities) such as Howard to educate and empower their communities when other state-run White institutions refused. HBCUs and their surrounding neighbourhoods are often like an island: a pocket of safe space for African-American students to learn, grow and begin to forge their own identity free of the White gaze. But over the past few years, the Black working class neighbourhoods around Howard became Whiter and more prosperous. The new locals began jogging, picnicking and walking their dogs on Howard University's historic green spaces and pathways. Some White locals would even walk on the running tracks during the same time as the school's track teams, which disrupted their daily practices. White families would eat lunch on top of famed plots marking the site where several Black fraternities and sororities were founded. The plots of land marking the founding of these fraternities and sororities were sacred – private areas often reserved only for members of those groups. When pressed about having more respect for Black spaces and understanding the unique history of HBCUs, many White residents scoffed and wondered why they needed to show any reverence. They viewed the university as public land like any other park or greenspace. The conflict escalated when Black students began protesting White presence at sacred sites around campus, calling the White people 'colonisers'.

Tracina nudged me in the direction of our towels and clothing, which were still in Beard Man's canoe, and we swam towards them. Once we reached the canoe and the edge of the pier, Beard Man beckoned us over, bent down and extended an arm to help pull us up. He then grabbed our clothes and towels from the canoe with a forced grin and we strode right through the brewing conflict. An older and thin ni-Vanuatu woman, dressed in a cyclone of purples and oranges and reds, motioned us into one of the bowlegged huts to change out of our wet swimsuits. She wore a huge peach-coloured flower in her hair. I let Tracina go first, not wanting to miss the ongoing argument.

The Gut ripped off his cap, bald shimmering head exposed, and stepped between Skinny Camera Man and Pale Woman. 'No more pichas! Pay! Pay or leave! Please!' he demanded, his stretched waistband clinging to his torso. Ni-Vanuatu-featured faces materialised from the land around me, their hair fashioned in locks, afros, beads, shells, cornrows and Bantu knots. There were wide noses nestled within thick beards, sloping foreheads and blotched eyes. Fluorescent bushes released brown bodies in brilliantly patterned floral and animal printed skirts. I wondered if I was only seeing the gathering crowd as some weird native fairy-like creature tied to the land… like in that movie *Ferngully*. A few years back, I'd heard an Indigenous Elder on Australian television saying, 'I belong to this land', and it struck me as both powerful and foreign to my own experience as an African-American descendant of slaves. I saw the same theme here of land and belonging, but I worried that my outsider gaze came across as a clumsy description that equated Black people to trees and dirt.

Looking around at the gathering of various shades, I imagined how I would describe this tapestry at my old barbershop in North Carolina. Food was often likened to skin colour in our African-American community in the South. We would have identified the ladies emerging from huts following the commotion as 'mocha' and 'caramel'. Meanwhile, the kids racing up and down green hills and into ditches around the blue hole would have been identified as 'peanut butter' and 'cinnamon'.

About a dozen bearded men gathered around me, pointing and whispering about the strangers who wouldn't pay. They were all about my height, which was average, and mostly on the skinny side, their faces and chests covered in thick hair. Sweat stains darkened their grey, black and eggshell T-shirts and singlets. Many held machetes, a tool commonly used to beat back brush on the island.

Tatted Man was unwavering. He stared them all down, licked his lips and clenched his meaty fuchsia fists. 'We won't pay. You don't own it.'

The ni-Vanuatu men began tapping their machetes on the barks of the trees, the wood singing out their warning. Tracina's dreadlocked head poked from behind the hut's curtain. Her large brown eyes darted around the landscape and she mouthed to me, 'Time to go?'

I smirked and tipped my head towards the crowded dock. Our guide, Beard Man, was preoccupied, gesturing wildly at the Europeans and yelling at The Gut in their local language. The Gut yelled back, his waistband releasing and the full avalanche of his stomach rolling down.

Tracina emerged from the hut wearing a soft pink sports top and black leggings. I could see the alarm on her face as the tapping around us quickened. It echoed across the forest and pulsated in my head like blood racing through an eardrum.

Pale Woman was now sheepishly hiding behind the men, her burgundy bottom lip quivering. She covered her bosom with her hat while the men took turns yelling back at Beard Man and The Gut in English. Each of them would then laugh, throw their hands up and say something to each other in their harsh native language.

The tapped trees shivered, emerald green crowns blocking out the sun. Machete blades left dark scars on their bark. Further up the trunks, I spotted the same gnarled tumours from the ones along the river, sprouting their claws and slowly descending.

'They're... god... they're everywhere.' Tracina clutched my arm, squeezing it red. She retreated into the hut, pulling me in with her. I left the curtain open and saw one crab, darker and hairier than the others, hover near Tatted Man's massive balding head, its mouth a wiggling mass of feelers and saliva. Suddenly, it leapt from the trunk, a surprisingly agile move for its size. Claws and pincers spread out wide, it landed on Tatted Man's forehead, its heavy shell making a cracking sound against his skull.

The thunderous tapping on the trees around us gave way to screams from him and the other Europeans. 'Get it off me! Fuuuuck!' Tatted Man wailed, grasping the shell and stumbling around in circles, sending drips of scarlet in all directions. Pale Woman burst into tears, pleading for assistance from the ni-Vanuatu as the other two men in her party tried to wrestle the crab off Tatted Man's head.

Beard Man gave me a broad smile as more crab spiders reached the ground and scurried towards the Europeans with pincers snapping. Santo's waters lay still.

ACTS OF FAITH

Meyrnah Khodr

AN ACT OF CHARITY IN ISLAM

Loose and easy with my head tilted to the side and teeth escaping, I start my day with a smile. I smile as I walk down Rickard Road. I smile as I'm shopping. During Bankstown Central's lunch-time rush, I smile at the middle-aged Asian lady behind the sushi counter with round glasses and a neat bun. I keep smiling when she ignores me and then serves a blond, freckly teenager who walks up to the counter several minutes later. *Smiling is charity*, I remind myself.

Late afternoon, the news on the radio counts the death toll in an attack on a masjid. Inside, I cry. I stop at the traffic lights and an Aussie lady with a tight perm rolls to a stop beside me in her beat-up Land Rover. She pokes her short and pudgy middle finger in the air. I force myself to smile at her. Down the road, an old man in a business suit with his pink skin bright in the evening light stops to check his mailbox. He yells at me as I drive past, 'They should have shot more!'

Jaw strained and eyes tight, I smile. 'Wallahu yuhibu asaabireen – And Allah loves those who endure patiently.'

AN ACT OF HATE ON ISLAM

Details assault my phone in rounds. Four dead. Brazen attack. Video footage. Rumours. Hearsay. Conjecture.

Poppoppoppoppoppoppoppoppoppop.

Lunch stretches slowly around relaxed laughter and microwaves groaning. Jenny offers me some quinoa salad. I decline, grateful I am fasting. My throat is too tight to swallow.

'Did you hear the news?' I ask Lisa and Jenny, slipping my question in between lesson plans and staffroom gossip. 'A gunman in Christchurch, at least four dead.'

Jenny nods, a blonde second of sympathy.

At home, we watch the numbers increase and my son pulls at the wiry strands of his beard as he tightens his plump lips and asks, 'How can he do that?'

I answer, 'Privilege.'

'But there are still some people who like Muslims, right?' my youngest whispers. Her thick black eyebrows slant upwards like hills, half-hidden under a messy fringe.

'Inna lillaahi wa inna illayhi raajioon – We belong to Allah and to Allah we return.'

AN ACT OF ADVICE IN MOTHERHOOD

My son,
Stay in the Area.
If you leave the Area, try not to look like a terrorist.
Shave that beard, it's just easier.
Don't carry backpacks –
Don't carry backpacks in crowded spaces like Bankstown Central.
Drive slowly and follow traffic rules.
Expect to be pulled over by police anyway.
Try not to sound like you're from Bankstown.
You don't need to call everyone bro and cuz.
And get rid of that mouth full of manoush.

ROUND EYES WHITE ASIAN

Adam Phillip Anderson

ONE

'Aw, go back to Indochina, ya ugly fucking gook.' Mark's rat-face stretched into a smirk.

'I'm Indonesian you dumb farmer cunt. And that word doesn't rhyme with book.' My heart tripled its tempo and my hands quivered.

Mark's weather-bashed skin was coarse and spotty like an old rockmelon – a sun-dried schoolboy. 'Aw, how the fuck would you know? Your dad's Aussie. You're not even that Asian.'

TWO

The lounge room smelled like salt and vinegar chips. I elbowed my way through bodies in the dark, the thick carpet under my Kmart dress shoes felt like a crime. A hi-fi stereo was playing 'Swimming Pools' so loud the bass rattled my vision. Boys in short sleeves took swigs of booze every time Kendrick Lamar said, 'Drink'. I poked some dude in his fuzzy blond forearm. He swung his nose around like a livestock gate, glancing at the air above my head then lowering his bloodshot eyes to meet mine. 'Have you seen Siena?'

He pointed at his can. 'I think it's vodka.'

Sighing, I backed away, shuffling and pivoting out the front door. My arms and neck tensed. *Fuck this suit and tie and all these people pretending they're going to give a fuck about each other after we finish the HSC*. I sat on the grey stone steps. *Where is Siena?* I thought about the hours I wasted listening to her problems: 'Can you believe Dad will only buy me a car if I pass my viola exam?' and 'I can't decide on Europe or America for my gap year,' and 'Which Pandora charm should I get next?'

A water feature on the manicured lawn made me want to urinate. I looked back inside at the sweaty scrum of limbs and cotton. Maybe a sneaky piss somewhere else? When I stepped into the street, I found Siena and my heart dropped into my intestines. She was sitting in the gutter in her red one-shoulder dress making out with a girl with a rave shave and no shoes. I stood and stared at the jet-black soles of the girl's feet for a moment before I took the pink rose off my jacket and threw it at them. As I walked away, I heard the shoeless girl say, 'Do you know that Japanese guy? He's kind of cute.'

THREE

The door had chipped off-white paint and a sticker stating: *Don't blame me, I voted for The Greens.* I knocked not knowing who was going to answer. Opening my phone, I re-read the text: *Yo sorry for being a dropkick but I've been sneeze vomming all morning, can you bring me some food? No pork or beef plz.*

In my other arm, I cradled a paper bag of pad kee mao, hoping the chilli and basil would help with his flu. Still no answer. I checked out the Honda CB125 parked in the street. The bike's mirrors poked out above the headlight like a one-eyed rabbit. The door squeaked open and a person with a septum ring, pink freckled skin and a self-cut Tool singlet stood in the frame. They eyed me up and down then snatched the paper bag from my arm. 'What the fuck? This has chicken in it! I'm a vegan! You're getting one star! I'm not paying for this!'

My eye twitched, brain struggling to relate these statements:

'I—Buh—Whuh.'

An engine groaned behind me. Suzuki 110 pulled up beside the Honda. A lanky Desi dude stepped off the scooter and zipped open his delivery backpack. 'Which one of you is Damien?'

I grabbed the bag of noodles back and said, 'So... is Adesh in his room?'

FOUR

In the distance I saw a Holden station wagon, white with one red door, turn into the street. I dawdled beside the sticky road, crunching gumnuts and jacaranda seeds under my Converses. My Labrador zipped left and right, frantically sniffing this and scent-marking that. The car's belts squeaked as it rolled closer. The driver had wraparound sunnies and a Bintang singlet. Windows down, the bare-rimmed wheels grinded on the asphalt. Next to him sat a guy with sunspots so big he looked like a moulting seal. I looked down at the footpath, minding my own. 'Oi. Jackie Chan! Don't eat that dog ay!' His mate cackled through his nasal passage.

My dog perked up his ears, snarling at the car's missing rear bumper. I yelled back through cupped hands as they drove off, 'Oi fuckstick, my dad's White!'

CASA SENDAS

Guido Melo

On the fifth day of every month, when my father collected his salary, the same thing happened at my house. My father, a proud Black sergeant for the Brazilian Air Force with short black hair and thick myopia glasses, arrived at home just after sundown. He was dressed in his usual ragged jeans and looked very sweaty with droplets on his forehead. I remember the bags under his eyes. I could never be sure if he was tired from his long shifts at the air base or just getting old. My father placed his tattered brown leather bag on the living room table. Frowning and looking at me from above his glasses, he said, 'Are you coming or what?' I nodded profusely, lips flat, attempting to hide my joy. It was supermarket day!

In 1989 Brazil, we needed to buy everything on the day my father's salary came in because of hyperinflation – a rampant type of inflation due to bad management of the economy by the defunct military dictatorship. If not, by the next day, the prices would hike and we would not be able to afford the monthly groceries and supplies that our large family required. I didn't understand the economy but my father explained to me that unscrupulous business owners raised prices on salary day to increase their profits. As the population purchased items, prices remained high. Next month, as salaries lost their buying power, everyone got a raise – generating further inflation.

My father said it was good for me to come shopping because my skinny ass could gain some muscles carrying bags and bags of items. But I remember thinking he was also happy that I was bigger and therefore could help out too. We always went to the same place, Casa Sendas Supermarket.

When I was about ten, my father took me to the local swimming pool. As we walked there, I remember how he held my shoulders softly and looked into my eyes. He said, 'When we are on the streets, you ought to do exactly what I tell you.' I remember thinking about what kind of situation would be so extreme as to warrant such devotion. So I questioned the severity of it. He then continued, 'If you are unsure, ask questions at home. But on the streets, if I say "run", you don't ask "why", you run.'

From then on, I followed his commands like a soldier. When we were out, my parents trained me to be hyperaware. I knew there was trouble when my mum held my hands and lifted her eyebrows. My father was blunter. If there was trouble, he just said my name in a deep baritone. My mother chanted a mantra when we would cross the street: 'A bruised soul is better than a body full of bullets.'

My father also coached me on what to say in case of danger: 'I am the son of Sergeant Andrade from the Third Communication-Air.' He emphasised that I needed to say these words as fast and as precise as possible when faced with trouble from the police, which was a regular occurrence for Black Brazilians – I'd seen the police ruffling up older boys sometimes just because their afros were deemed too big.

One day after school, I had to pick up my mother's medicine near the supermarket. Despite the fact that I had never been there alone and figuring I was old enough to take care of myself, I decided to venture into Casa Sendas. As I entered, I could smell the bread freshly baked. The warm dough and the noise of cheese slicing reminded me of breakfast, which was my favourite meal of the day. I looked up and noticed the lights were a bright blue-ish neon, just like a siren.

I browsed up and down every aisle deliberately and slowly. The meat section was cold and refreshing and a pleasant contrast to Rio de Janeiro's thirty-five-degrees-melting-everything-outside day. I walked up and down past the shampoo section. It smelled like flowers and coconuts, just like my crush Simone's long black hair. Sometimes in class, when she walked in early that morning, the whole room smelled like a floral paradise. I am sure everyone loved it just as much as I did because no one ever said anything to her.

The toy section was the most colourful, with items stacked from top-to-bottom. The biggest section was filled with Playmobil dolls. Some of my White friends had them. When I got invited to their homes, which did not happen often, I played with Playmobils for hours. Otherwise, it was back to the soccer field, where my skills did not require a price tag. If I were rich, I would buy the fireman and the Formula 1 sets. Looking at the boxes, I could imagine holding the toys in my hands, as if I was playing with them in my own house. I could be in that place for ages without noticing that was for sure! Mum and Dad always sped me up out of this section because we could not afford such luxuries.

As I was squatting on my knees, reading every description on the toy boxes, I felt my ears starting to burn. Was I being watched? The temperature dropped, the lights above seemed to be dimmed and the air changed, shifting the mood. First, I only sensed *him*. My shoulders deepened and I felt heavy. From the corner of my eyes, I noticed a segurança, a Black man but light-skinned. Much lighter than me. He was in his mid-thirties wearing a chequered red and white shirt and old ragged jeans like my father's, staring at me. I could feel my throat drying. I could hear my heart pumping rapidly like a samba. My mother's chants swarmed my head. He must have been thinking I was shoplifting. I was faced with a dilemma. If I made fast movements to leave, he would assume I was stealing. If I stayed quiet, he would continue to look at me and assume I was about to steal. Either way, he would frisk me. This was stamped from the beginning and whatever I did, I would lose.

Seguranças were like bounty hunters. They worked to protect, at all cost, the mostly White business owners of the town. Black-owned business perhaps existed, somewhere, but I was yet to see one. Like their 'cousins' in Mexico, the sicarios, the seguranças were the rogue operators of death. They had a de facto licence to kill. They saw themselves as vigilantes – as the good guys. They supposedly worked in the name of business owners and the traditional Brazilian family. But to me, they were the enemy. They hunted Black boys for sport. We all knew instinctively to be out of their way. Even my father's air force position schtick wouldn't have worked on them. Because my father was a sergeant and most of the military police were corporals, if the police stopped me, despite all atrocities, they would follow the hierarchy and let me go. Bounty hunters however, listened to no one.

I glanced side-eyed at the segurança. He placed his hand on his waist where he probably kept his gun holster. I was drawn to look straight into his eyes. He would not hesitate to fire at me right there and then. We both knew if he did this, he could get away with it. There is a thing with power – when you truly possess it, you don't need to act for others to fear you. The segurança's eyes were bloody with fire. I froze like a defenceless animal. He came closer and pointed to my waist. With his palms facing up, gesturing his hands like lifting an invisible weight, he told me to raise up my T-shirt. Not satisfied with humiliating me, he then pointed to my pants. 'Show me that,' he said. I lowered them until he could see my crotch.

'Pity you did not steal anything today... I was hoping I could give you a good bash,' he said with a smile on his face. My heart was trying to escape my chest. I felt the eyes of other shoppers on me. The segurança said, 'Get out of my face and don't you ever come back!'

As I walked out of the store, I knew what most of the adults inside were already thinking about me; that I was just a low-life negrinho thief up to no good.

SYDNEY ASIAN LIMERICKS FOR SELECTIVE SCHOOL GIMMERICKS

(WITH APOLOGIES TO THE FACEBOOK MEME PAGE)

Janette Chen

There once was a Chink that cleaned pools,
who heard he steals jobs from a tool.
His daughter named Betty,
got mad and got petty
and stole the top marks at her school.

—

The school is a swamp full of Asians
all trained in complex calculations.
Half the kids are Chinese,
they all want med degrees,
but Betty wants world domination.

–

After school Betty takes extra classes
in the subjects she's already mastered.
Though her marks are at peak,
she is here every week
for the cute NSB with the glasses.

–

For young Betty, the future looks bold.
For her parents, one thing to uphold;
'Old country: we starved.
New country: work hard.
Get a job: don't go hungry or cold.'

–

A top job after all the top scoring;
for Betty the emails are pouring.
Six figure pay pack.
She gives the job back.
Says, 'Fuck it, this shit is so boring!'

Bonus alternate ending:

In the day, Betty works for the bank.
In the night, Betty parties at Sanc.
Drink bubble tea,
make out with LBs;
a sweet life! For all this she gives thanks.

JUST BROKEN

Riley Ingersole

As I was getting ready to walk into my new school some Year 6 with brown hair and massive hands stopped me at the gate. He asked, 'What background are you?'

I replied, 'My dad's Aboriginal and my mu–' He cut me off and quickly replied, 'Then why are you white?' and I just didn't know what to say and then he said, 'Does that mean you are a thief?' and I was just broken.

I didn't go to class at all that day. I just walked home, close to breaking out in tears. My dad started screaming, 'Why the f**k aren't you at school?' He was massive with tan skin and a big body. He had a massive patch on his leg that looked like corned beef. I told him that Jacob was saying that I'm not Aboriginal and he gave me a hug, which felt like I was being wrapped up in a blanket, covering me completely. Dad said, 'I'm sorry people are like that.'

My dad grew up in Airds in multiple different houses. When he turned thirteen, he was given a challenging decision: he had to choose to either go to Queensland with his mother or stay in Airds with his father and he was frustrated because he knew his mother thought he would decide to go with her, so he decided to defy her thoughts and stay with his father. He ended up regretting that decision because his father was always drunk all the time and always hitting him so from the age of fourteen to seventeen, he lived with his grandmother, which would be one of the best choices of his life. He adored her, idolised her.

I returned to school the next day and found my teacher in the classroom. She was short with long black hair, dressed in what would become her usual black cardigan with pink shirt and black pants. I told her that Jacob was calling me a thief and saying cause I was white I couldn't be Aboriginal. She told the principal at lunch with a crazy Aussie accent, saying that Jacob was disrespecting me by telling me that I'm not Aboriginal.

After his suspension, Jacob ended up confronting me about it with eyes as wide as a pool ball with a brown iris. He spoke with his mouth barely opening. I was questioning my hearing ability because it sounded like he was talking as if he was speaking normally. He pushed me into an alleyway in the school that led to a dead end and tried hitting me with a big swing; wingspan of an eagle. It felt like time froze and I was sitting there thinking: *What will getting hit feel like from someone my age? Will it hurt or is he weak and he just acts strong because he has a height advantage?*

But his friend Danny, who was a bit taller than Jacob with even bigger hands, stopped him with a loud smack! Danny's hands were red with white fist marks in the middle of them. I was astonished. A million thoughts flooded my head: *Why did he do this? Isn't he Jacob's friend? Why would he risk hurting himself to help me?*

Danny yelled, 'What are you doing?' Jacob screamed, 'Hitting the little c*nt!' Danny replied, 'But why?'

'Because he's a fu**ing snitch.'

RECEIPTS

Sydnye Allen

ALDI

Bananas are the first thing I see walking into ALDI. Having forgotten snacks, I grab two small bright yellow ones and go to the register. I place them in a bag so my nervy two-year-old can eat without dropping banana flesh out of his stroller.

$1.07. I tap my card and wait for the receipt to be handed to me. I fold and slide it to the bottom of the plastic bag. My friend was fined for letting her daughter eat a yoghurt pouch before paying.

I trace the aisles as quickly as I can to collect the items on the list in order of proximity. Green bananas. Raspberries. Beef mince. Sausages. Salted butter. Yoghurt pouches. Walker-size nappies. Corn Thins. American peanut butter. Couscous. Frozen spinach. Belgian waffles. Seeded bread.

$37.43 later, everything is stuffed into a crumpled blue IKEA bag. The straps cut into my skin. I know I will have bright red striations on my shoulder. I walk out with the receipt tucked into the left cup of my bra.

COLES

Coles has the one item I couldn't buy at ALDI. Master Foods Garlic & Herb Seasoning – $2.25 on sale. I tap the card on the screen. I wait for the receipt to roll out and tear it off the dispenser from left to right.

'Excuse me… mmmmmm mmmmmmm,' says the fluorescent-vested COVID marshall. The only audible words are 'excuse me'.

'Excuse me?' I ask right back.

'Did you buy those other items here?'

I snatch the receipt from my bra pocket, hold it in the air for two seconds and keep moving.

I got receipts.

HARRIS FARM

Harris Farm stocks items year-round. All I need is one large jalapeño for homemade pico de gallo.

Raspberries: 2 for $5. I throw two punnets in the trolley, even though I know that the small font at the bottom of the sign reads: *Or $2.50 each*. On the way to the peppers, my toddler entertains himself by eating 'wasbewwies' off his fingertips.

The masked teenager with a long ponytail asks me, 'Do you have a bag?'

'Yes, I do.' I point to the crunchy blue bag on my shoulder.

'$7.36. Tap when you're ready.'

I tap and wait for the green tick on the machine. While I'm putting the card away, she asks, 'Would you like a receipt?'

'Yes, please.' I take the long receipt from her gloved hand and say, 'Thank you.'

I reach my hand in and release the punnets – loose jalapeños and receipt into the bottom of the empty bag.

WOOLWORTHS

Every Wednesday, I receive an email from Woolworths telling me how much I can save because their algorithm knows I only shop there for half-priced items. It's disconcerting to me that people routinely pay full price. The bold font email alerts me: *You can save $30.25 with this week's specials.* I am sceptical because they often suggest forty-packs of Solo to me after I once bought four bottles for a birthday party.

Biozet Attack Plus Eliminator and Arnott's Cracker Chips are half-price. Woolworths Leichhardt is the closest location. Bulk-buying requires a trolley. I choose one of those slimlines for people who don't have children to push. I line three boxes of Biozet at the end of the trolley. The corner on one is crushed so I put it back on the shelf. Three is too many anyway.

Then I push over to the snacks aisle. There they are, sea salt flavoured crackers that crumble like chips in the black box that has double front packaging. One side is upside up and the other is upside down, so I have to read the end that says *This End Up* each time I open a box. Saliva pools under my tongue. Eight or ten? They are $2.25. I make two rows of four boxes in front of the detergent.

Self-checkout has two available registers. I go to the compact *Card Only* one and start scanning. In proper and subtle Aussie English, the machine asks, 'Do you wish to continue? This machine accepts card only.'

I tap *Yes* and scan the second box of laundry detergent, followed by ten boxes of crackers.

$40 is the total. I calculate in my head. Eleven times two is twenty-two plus two twenty-five times eight is... Two twenty-five times two is four fifty. Four fifty times four is eighteen. Eleven plus eighteen is forty. I tap *Pay Now*.

'Follow the pin pad prompts to finalise your payment.' The machine's voice sounds sort of like a news anchor's. What neighbourhood would she be from?

I hover my card over the Wi-Fi signal and wait for the next screen.

'Do you wish to print a receipt?' I press *Yes* with my index knuckle.

Printer Error displays on the screen in a rectangular box. 'Please wait for an attendant.' A red light flashes over my head.

I wave to the person in an elbow length sleeve uniform shirt. Their nose pokes over the wrinkled top of their blue and white mask.

'Do you need something?'

'The machine didn't print my receipt.'

'Do you need it?'

My eyes roll up. I study the oily coating on this person's straight hair.

'Yes. I do.'

A series of pop-up screens are cleared and a bar code is scanned while the printer roll is replaced. They wipe their nose on the back of their right arm then hand me a docket that reads across the top: *Reprinted Receipt*.

I strain trying to release my clenched jaw. 'Um, thank you.'

REJECT SHOP

We walk past the Reject Shop and my two-and-a-half-year-old runs inside the door, his curls bouncing as he bounds. 'Balloons!'

'Bubba, you already have a balloon. We don't have time. Baba is waiting for us in the supermarket.'

'I want a balloon!' The circular balloons on a stick cost $3. 'I want a balloon!'

'Okay! Which balloon? These are all flat. You don't need one that says, "You're 1!" or "18". Do you want this unicorn one?'

'No, I want this one.' He is holding a construction vehicle balloon that is partially inflated.

'Are you sure?'

'Oh, candy canes!' He sprints toward Christmas. I pivot, leap, grab him under the arms and hoist him into the air.

'No candy canes. Let's pay for this balloon. Baba is waiting.' When we get to the counter, he waves the balloon around in circles while the dark-haired attendant waits for more direction. 'We need to pay for this balloon.'

'Just this?'

I nod with raised eyebrows.

'$3.'

'Can these be inflated? Do you have any others?'

She pulls a door open below the register, then closes it, looks around behind her and says, 'No.' She places her hand on the card reader and says, 'When you're ready.'

Ready, I tap and walk toward the door. 'Come on, Bubba, we have to go.' He is still top-heavy, tumbling over my arm toward the register. I struggle to hold us up. 'No, Mama! Our ceipt! Our ceipt!'

I back step and affirm. 'Yes, Bubba. Our receipt.' We walk away with him holding the squishy balloon in his left hand and the receipt in his right.

CALM DOWN

Ayoub Jama

DON'T FUCKING SWEAR

'Yunno the Air Max 95!'
'Yeah!'
'I fucking swear don't get me started about the green one!'
'Can you just leave me alone!'
'Bro I trying talk to you be grateful!'
'Ok ok calm down!'
'Ok!'
'I know they're ugly and that's why I think they suit you!'
'You little bitch!'
'Calm down you do this all the time!'
'But never in that context!'
'Don't fucking say that!'
'Woah!'
'Woah!'
'Ay calm down!'
'Don't fucking swear!'
'Ay ay please!'

MY NIGGA

Me and my brother sitting there at the madresuh
My brother sees a young child
'Bro you see dat'
'Ooh damn'
'He got a handball'
My brother in a full sweat
'Go get it'
'Nah you want it'
'Ok I'll get it lazy shit'
Mumbles under his breath
'Ay wanna give me that ball'
'Yes'
'So much gratitude is given to you'
Me laughing
'You look like you worship him'
'Shut up at least I got it'
'Ok'
'Let's play and I'll beat your ass'
Playing for the rest of break
'Oh it's at the end'
'No shit Sherlock'
'Lemme give him the ball'
'Ok'
'Suck a dick'
A random kid runs
He gives him the ball
'That kid's my nigga'

ACT LIKE A FILIPINO

Rizcel Gagawanan

I'm standing in the middle of a windowless studio with a blue screen propped up behind me. All the walls are adorned with framed movie posters, featuring the faces of the leading actors, who are White. The studio lights hanging above blind me. All I can clearly see is the camera and my scene partner standing next to it. She's a young twenty-something White woman fanning herself with the script. She seems well travelled, judging by the world map tattooed on her forearm. The tattoo looks like fairy bread where the 100s & 1000s beads are scattered over Europe. South-East Asia has some outlier dots, but there are no dots on the map of the Philippines. Tattooed right next to the map are some Chinese characters. They probably mean 'chow mein' instead of 'adventure'.

Chow Mein Adventure fans herself more vigorously. She looks to the ceiling, like the heat of the lights are getting to her even though she's on the shadier side of the room.

We begin the first take of my audition. In between phrases she lets out long sighs: 'Nurse Lopez... and Nurse Ramos... get... back to work. If you two... are going... to chit chat... in a language... other than English... you... do that... on your time.'

She isn't even looking at me. This 'speak English' line is so redundant. I want to let out a big groan but I'm on camera. My jaw tightens. Chow Mein Adventure's low energy doesn't faze me. This shitty script isn't even an obstacle. I've done auditions like this many times. I'm a professional. I'm confident and focused, acting out the scene as I'm supposed to. I'm even enjoying myself. I talk back at Chow Mein Adventure with authority in my tone and my stance: 'Ma'am, I'm just doing my job as I'm told to.'

A deep voice with heavy vocal fry interjects our scene: 'Can you, like, make yourself sound more like a Filipino?'

My chest tenses and for a few seconds I have trouble breathing. I purse my lips and stream out air through my nostrils like I'm a bull about to charge. Just. Chill.

I squint towards the audition panel. The casting assistant is behind the camera. She looks like she walked off the set of *Grease*: jet-black hair neatly styled in victory curls, black cat-eye glasses, red and black polkadot halter neck dress and lipstick a bold M•A•C Ruby Woo.

Beside the casting assistant are three judges seated behind a long trestle table. The director is in the middle, leaning so far back on his chair that his hairy pale legs and tanned boat shoes stick out from the front of the table. He stares at his crotch, where he fidgets with his mobile. The boat shoes, crossed over each other, sway side-to-side. He tilts his head over to his left towards the casting director, who's taking notes on her MacBook. He leans forward and looks at her screen for a few seconds, looks back at her and gives her a quick nod like he's drawing the Nike tick with his chin. Then his attention is back on his crotch and for a split second the whites of the CD's eyeballs poke out. She looks the busiest of all three, sitting upright, typing frantically and eyes fixated on her computer screen.

On the director's right is the assistant director, Brad. He's Brown! His nose is wider and flatter than mine and the acne craters on his cheeks remind me of my kuya (when we were kids, I called him Kuya Pizzaface). The tension in my chest deflates. But it's short-lived as I realise that Brad's glaring at me from his peripheral vision. He raises an eyebrow. Shit. I've wasted the past few minutes gawking around the room. He slowly turns toward me, repeating his original request: 'Can. You. Make. Yourself. Sound. More. Filipino?'

Brad wears a red flannel shirt buttoned all the way up and over it, a gold chain necklace with a gold crucifix. His sleeves are rolled up and his forearms are filled with tattoos of the same images on my mother's altar at home: Mother Mary with Baby Jesus, the Holy Family, the bloody face of Jesus wearing the Crown of Thorns and the praying hands holding rosary beads. The Filipino boys I grew up with had the same kind of tattoos. These were the dudes who acted like wannabe cholo gangsters. Brad dresses like a cholo but talks like a Becky.

The director's mobile is now at chest height and he's swiping up on the screen with his index finger, his face scrunched in concentration. Brad looks over to the director and the director nods at him to continue and goes to his *Pokémon Go* game. 'We envisioned that this character had come from the Philippines so she wouldn't have an accent like yours. Your voice sounds too...' Brad's hands are crab claws snapping at each other, '*Aussie*.'

The crab claws point at me like it's an accusation. Maybe he's right. I was born in the Philippines and moved to Australia when I was four years old. Maybe I'm too Australian to sound 'Filipino'. *Cool mate, if I sound 'too Aussie' then you're fucking Chris Lilley in brownface.* 'Sure,' I say, giving him the tight-lipped polite smile that I give to difficult customers at my day job as a barista.

Brad tips his head to the side, his eyes slightly closed and the corners of his lips turned down as if he's saying 'good girl' to a dog.

The last time I did a 'Filipino' accent was a few months ago at my best friend Reni's twenty-third birthday party. I was impersonating the time my fifty-year-old mum saw me talking to my classmate Shane in the car park. 'No boyprend unteel you gradwait prom highscool – hindi, unibersidy!' she yelled at me as she drove with the car windows down so the outside traffic could hear our conversation. Her starched daster dress ballooned up on her lap from the wind. We arrived home and she got out of the car, still yelling at me, her body shaking in anger but her daster dress unmoving. In the impersonation, I acted out everything, exaggerating my mother's four-foot body convulsing like she was one of those car dealership inflatable tube men, and the daster dress shifting around her butt stiff like a sandwich board. My friends laughed because all our parents, especially our mums, were the same. They were so strict when it came to interactions with the opposite sex, for fear we would get pregnant if we breathed the same air as a boy. But when it came to our brothers talking to girls, they didn't even peep a complaint. One time, I dobbed to Mum that Kuya Pizzaface had a girlfriend – she just dismissed me and spoke proudly of Kuya like he won a Lifetime Achievement Award. I bet Brad's mum ruled by the same double standards.

The camera's red recording light flashes on and Chow Mein Adventure launches into her first line, this time at a more energetic pace and a higher pitch. In the scene, I once again adopt my mother's Filipino accent, tightening the back of my throat. My mouth opens wide, and my eyes, eyebrows and nose all move like they have a life of their own. 'I wus not near rajology. I wus in da demencha wahrd superbising da payshents.'

This doesn't feel natural at all. My chest is burning and my armpits are dripping with sweat. The camera lights prickle on my face and I look to the floor. My cheeks and ears feel hot. If my family saw my Filipino caricature, what would they think? Kaka hiya siya.

'That was much better,' says the director. His velvet baritone voice stuns me. He sounds like a voice-over from a Mercedes-Benz ad.

I look up and the director is leaning on the table, his mobile phone resting next to his right elbow. 'I liked how you used moments to point your lips at the people you were referring to, that's something Filipinos do right?' He places his hand on Brad's shoulder.

Brad nods with a cheesy grin, 'Yeah, my mum does that all the time.'

The director leans over to Brad and whispers something to him. They have a brief discussion between themselves about my performance. Looks like I got this. I just have to keep acting like a stereotypical Filipino with my heavy accent and lip pointing. *White people love that shit!* My jaw clenches so hard that I hear static.

'Can you speak Tag-a-log?' asks Brad. *What is that? The hashtag for a firewood delivery company?*

'My Ta-ga-log isn't great,' I explain. 'I learned from how my family spoke at home and watching TFC on TV.' My heart rate goes hectic. My translation skills are worse than a tourist speaking to native Filipinos armed with a Tagalog-English dictionary.

'Let's do the scene one more time but in Tag-a-log.' Brad sits poised on his chair, his whole body now squarely at me. The director reclines and the CD's eyes are still glued to her MacBook. At this point, I've had no interaction with her. Maybe she just needs to be a presence in the room without being present. She's probably catching up on emails. I look at Chow Mein Adventure. She stares at the ceiling, lost in a daydream. It looks like she's gone through this countless times with other auditionees. She sighs and clenches the script in her hand.

Wait a sec, does Brad understand Tagalog? If homeboy can't even pronounce Tagalog right, he probs can't understand or speak it, even if his mum is Filipino. I feel a tickle in the back of my throat and I let out a soft cough. 'Ummm... ma-ma-hilig... a-ko... t-tu-tuma-e saaa... ka-k-kalye...'

'Pardon? Can you say that again, sweetie?' the director's velvet voice stings me.

'Mahilig ako tumae sa kalye!'

Brad flicks through the sheets of script laid out before him on the table. He traces the lines of each sheet with his index finger, scratching his eyebrow with his other index finger. The director is now sitting up on his chair, his hands formed in a prayer and the tips of his fingers slicing his chin back and forth. His eyes are slowly sizing me up. Goosebumps form all over the front part of my body – from my forehead to my ankles. I feel exposed.

'Yes, exactly like that!' Brad says with hands outstretched above his head like he's an AFL umpire signalling game.

The director asks Brad if he understood what I just said. 'Of course,' Brad says, combing his hand through his greasy black hair. 'She just translated one of the character's lines in the scene.'

The director pats Brad on the shoulder and gives him a wink and a thumbs up. I can't tell if Brad is just playing along with my game or if he really didn't understand. Either way, it's clear he's bullshitting the director. This is the third audition for a Filipino nurse role that I've attended in my five years of acting. The casting brief *always* asks for 'Filipino nurses'. This time the story is about a large amount of painkiller medication that goes missing and the nurse manager interrogates the Filipino nurses in the ward to find the culprit.

Speaking in Tagalog doesn't make any sense here. Chow Mein Adventure's character, Nurse Manager Carol, is White and only speaks English. Why would my character speak to her in Tagalog if she can't even understand me? My character, Nurse Lopez, has recently moved to Australia and is working illegally to send money back to her family in the Philippines. How can a nurse work illegally in Australia? Who wrote this trash?

We go for a third run. It starts off smoothly. Chow Mein Adventure does most of the talking as she accuses Nurse Lopez of stealing the meds: 'Lopez, your name is the last signature on the storeroom's register at the time the medication went missing.'

In the beginning of the scene my lines are short. It's easy to translate 'no it was not me' to 'hindi ako nag nakaw.'

Then I say, 'Hindi kami lang na mga Pilipino nurses.' *Oh dear God, my translations are worse than Google Translate!* There is a long awkward pause because Chow Mein Adventure doesn't know it's her turn to speak.

Towards the end of the scene, Nurse Lopez is crying because she's afraid that she'll get deported if Carol gets the police involved in the investigation. I'm blubbering broken, senseless Tagalog and my hands are flailing about like I'm a flightless bird attempting to take off. 'No – I mean, hindi ako yun! Wag mo-ninyo eee kunin-hindi-eee ta-wag yung police di-to.'

I feel like an uncoordinated busker singing off-tune and dancing my ass off for loose change. My emotional state has made my voice sound more Aussie than Filipino. I envision my mother hitting herself on the forehead, asking herself where she went wrong in raising me. The wires in my brain disconnect and thrash about. I'm not in the right mindset to automatically switch from English to Tagalog and back again. I don't have time to turn on my Tagalog brain – I've been on English brain by default my whole life. Chow Mein Adventure even talks over me and speaks faster like she's in a rush to get this over and done with, 'Idon'tknowhowthissituationwouldbehandledwhereyou'refrombut thisisaseriousmatterthatshouldinvolvetheauthorities.'

I squeeze in my 'mahilig ako tumae sa kalye' line. Even if Brad is a bullshit artist, I'm one as well. I have to cover my own ass first. No one else in the room can follow what I'm saying so who's gonna believe this shit?

When we're done, all the faces behind the trestle table are looking up at me. The CD shuts her MacBook, her hands clasped over her mouth so all I can see is her furrowed brow. Brad's forefinger and thumb rub his chin. His face is frozen with only his eyes subtly darting at the director. The director clasps his hands behind his neck, gently nodding his head, lips wrinkled. 'Yes, that's exactly how I envisioned this scene would go when I wrote the screenplay,' the director says with his right hand now on his heart, 'I just didn't have the words in Tang-along to authentically say it and you've done it for me.'

I'm disgusted with myself. I could say anything in 'Tang-along' and he'd buy it. The director continues with a monologue about his self-discovery sabbatical in Asia, which inspired him to write this film featuring a majority Asian cast, proclaiming it would be good for diversity on Australian screens. 'This scene in particular derives from my time in the Philippines where I witnessed so much suffering and hardship and such poverty, so much poverty! I'm sure you know this. I admire the resilience of the Filipino people and I wanted to depict their plight in an Australian context.' He sounds like a World Vision ad. I look over to Brad, who's staring at the table, smiling to himself and nodding, as though he's a marionette and the director is controlling his strings, making him dance to his tune.

—

Years later, I find out that the film went straight to DVD in Australia but had a short theatrical release overseas. I'm reminded about it when my cousin in the Philippines sends me a YouTube link of a bootleg copy of the film. I invite Reni over for a hate-watching session. She arrives at my house and we're wearing the same Corgi-patterned pyjamas we bought together when we chased the end-of-year sales last month. She brings my favourite Moby chocolate snacks and some leftover kaldereta and biko that her mum, Tita Flor, made for dinner the night before. We stream the YouTube video on my TV screen and dim the lights in my lounge room so we have a full cinema experience.

Twenty minutes into this ninety-minute fiasco, Reni says, 'Dude, isn't this your audition scene?'

It's been years and she still remembers. She's my go-to person for last minute audition prep. The actress playing Nurse Lopez is a mixed-race Filipina who looks like a carbon copy of all actresses in the Philippines: paper thin, Vicki-Belo-white skin with a straight-edged nose and long shiny straight black hair. She says in an American accent, 'Ma-he-leg a-ko too-ma-eh sah kal-yeah.'

I snort and choke on some rice grains from Tita Flor's biko. 'Girl!' Reni wields her fork in the air vigorously from side-to-side, flicking bits of biko everywhere. 'Did she just say what I thought she just said?'

We pause the video, move the timeline back a few seconds and play it again. 'Lol! They used my bullshit line!' I gesture my biko-laden fork at the TV and a rice grain hits the screen.

'Mestiza doesn't even know what she's saying! Play it again!' Reni laughs, kneeling on the floor.

We rewatch the scene several times until my abs cramp like I've done a thousand sit-ups. Reni is crying, completely bent over. Her cackling reminds me of Mum when she laughs hard, voice bellowing and filling the room, the sound starting off at a high pitch and then quickly going deep, tears in her eyes.

'Tu-ma-ha-eh sa-ha-sa-ha ha ha ha kalye!' Reni gets up from the floor and puts her hand on her crotch to check for wetness. 'Crap, I peed myself!' she says. 'At least I can admit that out loud, unlike shitting on the street and liking it!'

HIJAB DAYS

Amani Haydar

A big pig spins on a rotisserie, putting on a show for the insurance brokers, claims managers and actuaries my law firm is entertaining at the annual client Christmas party. It's the first thing I see as I step out of the elevator into the loud room. There are palm fronds on the wallpaper and art deco light fittings give off a warm glow. I can't stop staring at the pig. I don't like the look of it. Not because it's haram but because of the way it turns on the silver rod. It rolls in the air like it once rolled in a paddock. I feel bad for the pig even though it has been petrified and golden for some time.

People stand in small circles near the black marble bar or lounge on yellow chairs in dim corners of the room. After dark, the venue is a nightclub, somewhere I'd never go other than for a work function. We solicitors are expected to attend. This is before my hijab days. I straighten my hair. I wear Ted Baker and pearls and shoes that harass my toes into neat triangles. The client Christmas party is always fancy because the clients gossip among themselves afterwards about which firm celebrated best.

I greet a man, Sean, from one of the client's offices. I've been working with him over the past few months. His cheeks are pink and round and his beard is white. He looks like a man-sized lawn gnome. We're making small talk about a four-car pileup. The poor piggy has been shredded and it comes around in a tray of sliders. I raise a palm and say, 'No, thank you.'

Sean looks at me with wide eyes and says, 'Well, I'm going to have some!' He takes two sliders from the tray and eats them in three bites each. I try to go back to the four-car pileup but the client leans in too close when he talks and I find myself stepping backwards every so often to create a buffer between my eyes and his mouth.

I'm hungry but the other meal option is oysters. Waiters shuck them over a table of ice at the back of the room. Short wide knives gleam as they pry the wet shells open. I ask Sean about another case I know he's been working on but he is chewing. I wait for him to finish, taking a sip from my glass of cranberry juice. Sean finishes his last bite of food but instead of answering my question he sucks the salt and oil from each of his fingers – pop pop pop pop pop. He maintains eye contact, wanting me to know how good the pig tastes. Sean's fingers glisten as he grunts, 'Mmm.'

A man with brown skin and a dense moustache enters our conversation. He's wearing a badge with the name 'Mohamad' on it next to the sharp red-lettered logo of the company he's from. I haven't met Mohamad previously but Sean seems to know him. Sean nods, offering no introduction. I say hello and state my name while clutching my glass to avoid shaking hands. He is holding an orange juice.

How many other Muslims are in this room keeping hunger at bay with kid drinks? I wonder whether I should provide feedback to our human resources department about this. I don't really mind my dietary preferences being ignored but it's embarrassing not to feed the clients.

—

The following August coincides with Ramadan and a case I'm working on is being heard in the Supreme Court of NSW. It's a matter about a farm that grows more cotton than I can visualise. One evening, another solicitor and I are in conference with the barrister representing our client. We refer to him as Counsel. Counsel is a tall man with shaggy grey hair. An ex-politician. He owns the building we're meeting in – a heritage-listed federation-style building on Macquarie Street. Counsel's back and legs fill the square room we're in as he paces back and forth, reading from a textbook. Black robes and a curly wig are draped over a coat stand in the corner. We had court today and the hearing continues tomorrow. My colleague shuffles through papers while I take notes. I've been fasting all day but I don't take any breaks because I don't want anyone to think that my religion makes me lazy.

I watch the sky turn orange then darken through the window over Counsel's shoulder. He switches on a tall lamp and reads a section of legislation out loud for the third time. I say *bismillah* in my heart and lift my water bottle to my lips. I extract three dates from a Ziploc pack in my handbag. I place them in my lap on top of my binder. They're like garnets in the lamplight. I eat them one by one, silently, so as not to disrupt the conversation. Counsel stops reading, drops into a chair and crosses his legs so that his big brown shoe hovers in the middle of the room. He smiles and asks, 'Are you still doing that thing, Amani?'

I lower my half-eaten date with the pit poking out and brush a stray strand of hair from my eyes. 'Yes, I've been fasting for Ramadan,' I reply.

'Ah!' he exclaims, beaming. 'I have a case about some of your group who want to build their church somewhere and we're arguing section 116 – it's unconstitutional!'

Counsel's chair creaks as he uncrosses his legs and leans forward. None of what he has just said makes any sense to me. I nod, 'That sounds interesting.'

Counsel lifts a hand to his belly. 'But I wish I subscribed to Ramadan,' he says, rubbing his tummy and chuckling. 'Maybe I'd lose a little weight.'

—

On the train platform at Granville, I stand as far back from the edge as I can. I am pregnant with my second child and the smell of barbeque chicken, which usually makes my mouth water, today makes my head spin. I'm on my way to hear a friend's presentation about women's health in the city. I haven't caught the train since I took leave during my first pregnancy a year ago. My train arrives puffing warm smoky air into the folds of my hijab. I step carefully over the gap onto the train and, remembering that hot air rises, I waddle towards a seat on the bottom level.

The event goes well. I meet lots of women who are involved in interesting things: Tamil women who wear pink saris to raise awareness about breast cancer, Afghan women who run informative seminars for women refugees. The time passes quickly as I listen to them talk about their work. I leave with a lady who wears glasses at the tip of her nose and has her pale grey hair up in a neat bun. She works at one of the big charities. We're walking through the Devonshire Street tunnel when she asks me what I do.

'I'm a commercial lawyer but I've been on mat leave for a while,' I say, waving a hand at my belly.

Her eyebrows fling up to the top of her face and she asks, 'Where did you work?'

I reply, 'At a firm, here in the city.'

'Well, you'd have done a lot of good for the women in your community just by turning up,' she says, nodding at my hijab.

My throat stiffens at her words. 'I was a lawyer, not an activist,' I mumble in response. 'It was before my hijab days.' I'm about to elaborate when a busker wearing a poncho and a nose ring drowns me out with a strum of her guitar. Drops of sweat swell at my temple as the tunnel stretches on. We pass a man who flings out his arm and places a flyer in my hand. It reads: *Stop Sharia Law*. I fold the paper into a small square as I walk. The ink cracks and smudges along the creases.

A wave of nausea strikes as we pass the takeaway shop that sells chips and gravy, hot dogs and strips of pork crackling. When we arrive at the barriers, my companion suddenly pats me on the shoulder.

'Keep up the good work!' she says with a smile.

As my train takes off, I wonder what's become of my files since I left the firm and if I'll ever go back.

SUBTLE RANTS

Christine Shamista

FACEBOOK COMMENTARY

It sounds to me like ... maybe
he just meant ... look ... don't be
oversensitive ... I think
you were imagining ...
terrible ... appalling ... you should
definitely complain ... that
was a bit victim blamey ... how
dare you ... I'm married to
an African-American man ...
make sure you ... this is why
I hate people ... let it roll off ...
you can let it ruin your day ... or not ...
the choice is yours ... I think
it was okay to be upset ... but
do you really ... lots of White
privilege surfacing here ... I
would have ... welcome
to the life of a Brown person ...
I hope this doesn't sound
patronising ... but ...

WHEN I COULDN'T GET AN UBER

What have you been doing?
With whom? Where did you go?
Listen to this. Where are you from?
No, that's not what I mean. Where
are you *really* from? Oh, they used
to have good cricket players.
My friend's from Sri Lanka. Do you
know him? Look at the Christmas
tree. It has twenty different colours.
Tourists are everywhere. See
this shop window? To get the money
in. Migrants. Look at this taxi
driver – doing a U-turn here.
He's Indian. This year is quiet.
Business is slow. You hear this
on the news? They all lie. I had
this customer. See that?
We almost crashed! He almost
made me crash. I don't want
any more scratches on my car.
I like you. You're a good
customer. Take my card.
If you ever need a driver.

SOME WORDS

Krisneth Paddy

TRUMP

Yellow hair that looks like chicken noodles.
Fat neck roll that looks like a bum cheek.
Big stomach that looks like he is pregnant.

TWO FUCKS

The election was announced. I don't give two fucks about these cunts going at each other's neck. I don't care about Trump and Biden. I don't care Biden won. I just don't want him to involve us in a stupid war and plus Joe Biden will probably die of old age in three years. Just enjoy life you old fuck. Donald Trump is a yellow son of a bitch.

DROPPED AND BASHED

My first day in Kindergarten was a day I almost dropped and bashed someone. His name was Bully, I mean Billy.

So Billy just said, 'What was your name?'

I said, 'Krisneth.' This is when the bloody beef started.

He was like, 'Did you say Christmas bruhh?'

Then the teacher was saying to me, 'Go to the naughty corner.'

Then it was lunch; Billy started following me around saying, 'Christmas! Christmas!'

I was so mad I yelled, 'You White piece of shit!' and started chasing him.

He started running like if he saw a ghost. I was so mad that I could kick this White skinny boneless prick with yellow teeth and throw him at a brick wall and break his whole body.

Then my sister came and grabbed me and tried to calm me down. She whispered, 'It's okay!' Repeated it slower and quieter.

Then I remembered if I bashed him what will I achieve? What will I get? I would just get in trouble by words. Beat someone, injure someone, for just some words.

GHOST GIRL SUMMER

Ting Huang

'So, we have quite a lot of information about the inhabitants of Pompeii, even though it was wiped out almost two thousand years ago. Can anyone tell me something interesting they've learnt about this Roman city?' Ms Parks asked.

I wanted to cup my hands around my mouth and yell out, 'Did you know they had hundreds of, like, dick statues?' but my arms were heavy in the heat. And anyway, I was more interested by Ms Parks' mouth and the way it jumped around her face as she spoke, like a wrinkly red prune suddenly taking on a life of its own.

'Yes, Caitlin!' Ms Parks called out, jolting me.

I sat up straight and looked around. The B12 classroom at North Sydney Girls High was stuffy with the summer stench of twenty teenagers doused in Impulse body spray. In the back row, Caitlin had her hand all the way up. The charms on her Pandora bracelet jangled as she wriggled her arm. I could hear Hyun-hee and Lisa, the Koreans, chatting quietly to my left. Textbook paper rustles blended together with the faint whir of a ceiling fan that made me dizzy whenever I looked directly at it. I wiped my upper lip with the back of my hand.

'Most of the city and its inhabitants were actually really well-preserved under the ash from Mt Vesuvius,' Caitlin piped up, her wiry curls bobbing like a blonde cloud behind her head. If only it was a rain cloud of volcanic ash. I would have loved to see her catch on fire and turn into one of those freaky preserved plaster bodies, like in the photo projected on the smartboard. Ms Parks beamed in response; thin lips stretched taut over yellowed teeth. I nudged my friend Trish sitting next to me, accidentally clashing my elbow against her bony netballer arm, and rolled my eyes.

We knew Ms Parks enjoyed only two things during these hour lessons. The first was going off at me and Trish for some reason or another. 'You two done? Others are trying to learn,' she would say in a shrill voice that reminded me of a rabid poodle. A poodle I wanted to choke out. The second was fawning over Caitlin Ridley. All the teachers loved her, especially Ms Parks, who compared Caitlin to her daughter all the time. 'Oh, you're just like Keira, my eldest. She's at Newtown Performing Arts High School, you know! She's got a real knack for the theatrical, like you!' she'd say as I tried my best not to chunder.

Caitlin was a drama-kid, which meant she had been in every NSG musical since Year 7, which meant she got to play Sandy in *Grease* last year, which meant she was an annoying Skip bitch. And all the seniors knew Caitlin too, through her sister Hannah, who was currently school captain. I remember standing in the Great Hall a few years back on Orientation Day, scanning the blonde-headed portraits of past school captains lining the wall. Dad stood with me and laughed, clutching the soft mound of his belly, which stuck out from the rip-off Ralph Lauren polo he'd gotten from Flemington Markets.

He said in Cantonese, 'One day you'll be a school captain up there with all these gwei mui eh? Can you imagine that!'

I looked out at the other Year 7s, a sea of dark hair washing into the hall, and didn't say anything. I couldn't imagine any of us up on that wall. Last names like Kim, Kaur, Chen and Gupta weren't names made for the wooden plaque.

Somewhere in between Caesar's civil war and Pompeii's stone phalluses, Trish pulled her Sony Ericsson out from her grey Country Road tote bag. She flicked her overgrown black fringe out of her eyes and started typing. A Chinese jade charm dangled from her phone, the red tassel at the end bouncing as she pressed into the buttons. Trish leaned over to show me what she'd typed: *Can't train with you to Parra after school i'm meeting Amir at cwood*. My face grew hot. Catching the train home out West together was the whole reason we became friends in Year 7 in the first place. And this was the third time in a row she was dogging me for her flavour of the month, Amir – a guy who worked at St Leonards Macca's.

'How you gonna get back to Kellyville from Chatswood?' I whispered.

'I'll just tell Mum I stayed back late to study with you,' she said, pulling her hair into a high ponytail. Inky strands clung to her neck as she fanned herself, unconcerned. 'What's your problem?'

Trish only thought Amir was cool because he was in Year 12 and went to Chatswood High. The one time I ever met him, he spent the three hours bragging about how he got a gobby in the bushes at Blues Point last New Year's. He was definitely the kind of guy who'd get a mystery ATAR.

I couldn't help myself. 'Dude, Amir is such a fucking derro!' I said.

'Shhh.'

I whipped my head around. Caitlin was shushing me from the back row, her gaudy silver bracelet glinting as she pressed her finger to her lips. *Shut up, you bogan gronk-cunt!* I thought, glaring at her.

'Anything you'd like to share?' Ms Parks spat molten rock across the room.

'No, sorry,' I muttered. Trisha's head was bowed down, as though she was concentrating really hard on her notes. I saw little flecks of dandruff scattered through her hair like cinders. *And she thinks an older guy could ever like her back?*

'Good. If I hear one more word out of you, you'll be staying after class to do homework.'

I could hear my ears turning red. I tried to make eye contact with Trish but she was looking away. She was fingering her stupid Chinese phone charm, as if people couldn't already tell what she was just from her pancake-flat nose and thick box-framed glasses that shrunk her eyes down to pinpricks. Looking at the charm made me cringe. I wanted to grab it and throw it against the wall. Watch the jade smash to smithereens. 'Yeah, well NSGs do homework in their spare time anyway, so that's not a punishment,' I said, gripping tightly onto the side of my table.

Ms Parks narrowed her blue eyes. A vein bulged in her forehead. I wanted it to erupt from her skull. I imagined stabbing her in the throat so forcefully that the bun at the back of her head came loose. 'You girls won't make it anywhere in the real world, you know,' she finally said. 'All your type knows is study study study study. A fat load of good that'll do you out there.'

Sliiiiiiiiiiiiiiiiiiiiiiiit. Blood bubbling below. I exhaled. Any background chatter in the room had stopped. I felt shame come up from my stomach, burning white-hot into my chest. I stared at Ms Parks, pictured her gurgling and spluttering. Blood turned to lava, streaming down her neck to pool in the deep hollows of her collarbones. Her skin blistered over and over. Tiny exploding sacs sprayed pus on the smartboard behind her. I breathed in. Singed flesh filled my nostrils. I sat and waited for a moment – though I wasn't sure what for. *Will Ms Parks take back what she said? Is Trish gonna jump to my rescue?* I pushed against the edge of the desk and shot up, scraping the hind legs of my chair against the floor so that it screeched through the still air. Bolting towards the door, I heard Ms Parks declare, 'And that's detention for you!' as I ran through the hallway, down the stairs, out into the quadrangle.

The bell hadn't gone yet so there were only a few tartan-clad seniors sitting cross-legged on the ground. Probably memorising their physics notes or whatever. I honestly couldn't be fucked running into them. I started power walking towards the fence on the other side of the quadrangle. Klak kluk, klak kluk, klak kluk. My Payless Shoes lace-ups stomped sullenly on the pavement. I stopped at the edge of the school and turned to look back at the grounds. Its students were only dots now. Fuzzy little peppercorns that I could barely make out if I tried.

ZOOPER DOOPER

Heikmah Napadow

Brrrrrrring! The bell marked the beginning of recess. Classroom doors at Undercliffe Public School swung open with students flooding the main hall. Hop. Trot. Gallop. 'No running inside!' Mr Nolan's deep voice reverberated through the hall. Wanting to utilise every moment of our twenty-minute break outside, our tiny bodies bunched shoulder-to-shoulder as we shuffled our feet towards the green double doors.

Once outside, I skipped towards the school canteen located on the other side of the playground. My pleated maroon sports skirt fanned up-and-down as each of my feet kicked up in turn. *Mmmmm*. Saliva glistened on my lips, already tasting the exaggerated orange-flavoured Zooper Dooper. Mumma only gave me lunch money on Fridays, just enough to buy myself a sandwich or a meat pie. Each time she said, 'Remember to bring me back the change!' But she forgot to ask for it last week, so I had enough money to get myself a treat this time. One shiny twenty cent coin rested in my flattened palm.

'Orange Zooper Dooper, please!' All five fingers wriggled as I reached for the paper towel-covered frozen tube. Plastic wedged between my front teeth when I ripped it open while walking down the steps out of the canteen.

Each time I licked and slurped, the corners of my mouth turned upward. Jade, Mya, Riley and Sienna; the usual girls were playing a game of tag in the grassy area beside the canteen. Mya called out 'Bar!' – halting the game of tag before jogging towards me. The motion of her long black ponytail swinging from side-to-side like a pendulum clock made me clutch my short braid, which rested on my left temple. Mya's sports skirt stopped three inches above her knee. Triangular quad muscles contracted as she ran. One day after witnessing her arms and legs whipping through the air like propellers as she completed a series of cartwheels and somersaults, she told me, 'I started gymnastics when I was four years old and all my brothers play rugby.' Long wavy hair clung to the sweat streaming down her face and neck.

'Hey, wait up!' She reached out to me holding a piece of paper. 'It's an invitation to my birthday party, next Saturday.'

'For me? Thanks!' I snatched the invitation out of her hand to examine it.

My heart was pumping hard and fast as I read how I was invited to celebrate the tenth birthday of Mya O'Connor, which was printed in cursive letters. I lifted my head from the rainbow unicorn invitation to see twenty-eight of Mya's teeth aligned, grinning at me. I responded by smiling back with as many teeth as I could. *She really does want me to go to her party!*

'Ewww! Gross!' someone shouted, followed by the sound of them sucking in their teeth. Mya whipped her head around to investigate and her ponytail slapped me in the face. My head cocked to the side until it was almost parallel with my left shoulder and fixed on Jade standing a few metres behind Mya. Jade had both hands tightly rolled up into fists that she pinned against her hips. She tapped her foot so furiously that dirt stirred up around her. I studied her sharp jawline and thin wide lips, likening her to an alien. How did this short girl with transparent skin and a bulbous head framed by a blonde bob assume such power over the Year 4 girls? 'Don't invite her!' she said, speaking to Mya but directing her electrified green eyes toward me. Her right eyebrow lifted slowly as if it were being pulled by an invisible string, forming the shape of an upside-down tick. My face and hands pulsated and my entire body was stiff. My grip on the ice block tightened and I felt the cold burn my hand.

Mya shot back, 'Fuck off! I'll invite whoever I want!'

My eyelids exposed the white edges of my corneas. *Did she just use a swear word? And at Jade?* I'd never heard anyone speak to Jade that way.

Jade's head jolted back whilst blinking wildly as though each of the words Fuck. Off. I'll. Invite. Whoever. I. Want. had been rolled up into balls and physically launched at her. She clenched her jaw so tightly they bulged outward. She scanned my body, starting at my feet until her green eyes and my brown eyes locked in a stare-off. A drop of melted Zooper Dooper dripped on my hand and rolled onto the invitation. I looked down and licked the thawing fluoro liquid.

'Thanks, Mya,' I said, shoving my invitation into my right skirt pocket. I spun around in the opposite direction, pressing my hand against my chest as I took a long and deep breath in. Then while pushing the air out of my mouth, I closed my lips around the opening of the Zooper Dooper and took a bite over the plastic, breaking the ice block within. 'Mmmm!'

MAGIC PANCIT

Mark Mariano

'Who's that for?' I asked Mama as she prepared another helping of steaming pancit.

On the serving spoon, a piece of Chinese sausage wrestled with a shred of red cabbage. The Corelle bowl clinked as she placed it on the countertop, next to a tall lit candle. 'Your lolo,' she said, stretching out her free soy sauce-stained hand to caress my face.

I sat with her answer for a minute, pouting as I counted the hungry Filipinos at the 'special' dinner table. We had the regular two families over. They weren't related by blood but that stuff is always relative. The table setting wasn't fancy at all – it was just our dinner space with a bleached white table cloth and a giant fruit bowl. 'I only see Papa and all the other parents,' I said. *Did I forget to greet someone?*

'I know, anak,' my mother said, resting her hand on her chest. 'He's here.'

Mama prepared a feast on all of our birthdays. Two for the parents and five for the children. This one was for my older brother, Jared. I sat next to him; his bushy brows furrowed in impatience. At the centre of each spread was a colossal serving of pancit – we had it at every celebratory occasion. After a brief prayer from Papa, we all started to dig in. 'Tita Anna makes hers too salty!' my younger brother, Jerome, muffled as he stuffed his mouth. 'Oily too!' my older sister, Maricon, chimed in, with a little more eloquence. Mama smirked as she tended to our visitors. My titas and titos nodded in agreeance, knowing Mama's was the supreme dish amidst all the titas.

I zoned out the gossip and honed in on the mammoth serving Mama set aside for me. I licked my lips as I pulped two small calamansi wedges onto my packed plate; eyed the salty brown vermicelli strings as Jared handed me a spoon from the pile. Without waiting another second, I shoved a mini-mountain into my mouth, inhaling the sweet chunks of cured meat. I let the heap sit on my tongue, steam slithering out of my nostrils. I leaned back into my chair; my eyes clamped shut as I hesitantly swallowed. I packed another spoon, this time with pork belly. The hair on my arms stood as I brought this new heap closer to my lips. The noodles, drenched in sour calamansi, cut through the pork's greasiness. I felt the warm serving travel down, making itself home in my half-empty stomach. I chugged a cup of cold Sprite, prompting a roarous burp. Around me, a chorus of slurps and clinks crescendoed into a harmonious symphony; one even louder than my tipsy aunties on the karaoke machine.

The rest of that night, my head swivelled, scanning everyone's face for my lolo. The last I heard, he was back in the Philippines, tending to his small farm. I had only seen him in photos – often browned and blurry – but I knew his face. Better yet, I knew his curly coarse hair, as it was just like mine. My curiosity soon died down as I played with my siblings; an episode of *Charmed* had just aired and I was keen to test out the powers I knew for sure I had deep inside me. My Tita Anna-hating brother watched from the three-seater couch while I attempted to 'blow up' my dad's recliner. I clenched my hands in tight fists before spreading them wide open with gusto, expecting the chair to combust. Maricon and my only-child cousin,

Larein, giggled over their Nokia brick phones. 'Don't laugh at me!' I squealed at them.

I stomped towards the still-in-tact recliner, collapsing onto its brown leather with tightly folded arms. A tear scrolled down my scrunched face. Piper made it look so easy in the show and her sisters were always so supportive. The girls stopped giggling and I avoided their pleading eye contact at all costs, choosing instead to 'hmph!' at the beige wall.

'We're not laughing at you, Mark. We promise!' they eventually yelled in unison.

Larein carefully approached me, her footsteps sneaky and hushed. I turned to confront her and came face-to-face with her finger. She tickled my stiff nose, shaking me from my tight posture. Maricon pulled me in for a hug, showing me the corny text one of their crushes sent them: *I'm gonna kiss your face off.*

'Yuck!' I grimaced. I turned to nestle into Maricon's shoulder, my body still a little stiff from yelling at them. 'Want me to blow him up for you?' I asked, hoping it would make up for the tantrum.

After unsuccessfully searching for a leftover can of Sprite the next morning, I noticed the bowl on the kitchen counter in the same place. Jared sat across from the arrangement in his pyjamas chomping on a serving of cake. The candle was half its height and a big chunk of the pancit was gone. I felt a tap on my shoulder. 'Here, 'nak. Breakfast.'

Mama handed me a warm bowl – it was the missing chunk of pancit. 'Wasn't that for Lolo?' I asked, pushing it towards Jared.

'It'll bring you good luck!' Mama said, winking as she handed me a fizzing cup of lemonade.

—

'The flame, the pancit and the prayer,' Mum whispered, meditating almost, after I blew out my birthday candles in front of my aunties and uncles. 'Lord, we are thankful for the food that nourishes us and keeps us strong. Pa, Ray, Lolo, Lola, continue to keep us safe.' She lit the candle and arranged the dishes from largest to smallest, knowing our ancestors had their favourites. It had been a few months since Jared's birthday, where we offered a meal to our late lolo. I begged Mama not to do one for me, knowing now what it meant. She still went ahead, ignoring my pleas as she wiped noodle debris off the counter. 'This is how we honour them,' Mama said, tickling my chin, narrowly missing the sweat that pooled on the back on my neck. 'We celebrate another year of life, the good and the bad, with food and light, and we do it for them.'

'My friends are gonna think I'm weird!' I yelled. She planned to keep the pancit out the whole day. The fight was futile and it was too late – the girls were already starting to show up. Maricon answered the door, forcing a smile as Milly and Bianca rushed past the pile of shoes in our doorway to give me a hug.

I avoided eye contact with the setting the whole night. The aging plate of pancit had been sitting in the kitchen since the morning and it was starting to smell a little ripe. I prayed the girls didn't notice. Milly held her Uno cards in one hand and pointed across the living room with the other. 'What's that?' she asked, nodding towards the neat Corelle setting.

Mama emerged from the kitchen, almost as if she were waiting for this exact moment. This was it. This was the end of the world as I knew it. I just wanted to be normal. I wanted party pies and cans of Coke. I wanted a marble chocolate cake, not the sickly sweet purple one Mama picked up from the Filipino bakery down at Doonside Station. I fought back the tears that started to block my nose. I had to deal with my coarse curly hair, my patchy brown skin, and now this? My head burned as I rushed to find an explanation – one that didn't force me out as some loony magical freak to my regular friends. I couldn't think of anything.

'Ma!' I yelled. She had opened her mouth to answer Milly but shut it after scanning my scrunched face. Mama and I locked eyes – mine raging, hers defeated.

'I think the pizza's here,' Bianca whispered, cutting the tension.

Mama fished money out of her muumuu pocket, paying the delivery man at the door before carefully placing the food on the recliner next to us. 'Dig in guys!' she said in her unnaturally Aussie tone – the one she reserved for parent-teacher interviews. The Uno game fizzled as we nibbled away at our supreme pizzas.

I didn't care that it was good luck. I could handle the Halliwell sisters vanquishing demons every Sunday, but when I saw the offering on my birthday, my chest got heavy and my heart started to race. It was the same feeling I got whenever we drove past the cemetery on the hill in Prospect along the Great Western Highway. I spent every motorway drive with my arms stretched in the air praying that the superstitions were true, that smelly armpits scare away spirits. Ghosts creeped me out. Death creeped me out.

Celebrations were over and the girls and I stood on my porch, swatting away the mosquitoes that buzzed around the spring onions Mama planted in our front yard. We were pooped. A deflated pile of balloons slept at our feet, once filled with the helium that now lived in our lungs. A bright red Holden Commodore rumbled into our driveway. Milly's dad had arrived. I waved the girls goodbye and waited for them to turn the corner before slumping my shoulders and heading inside. Mama was washing the dishes. She faced the window as I glared at her profile. She paused scrubbing to wipe her forehead with her forearm, stopping a bead of sweat in its tracks. I grabbed a cloth and started to dry the spoons. The utensils clinked and clattered in my hands as water gushed out of the tap. 'I'm sorry about earlier, Ma.' I put the spoons away. Sudsy water splashed about in our little one-drain sink.

'When do you feel the most love, anak?' Mama said as she squeezed more soap on her tattered dish sponge, honing in on the behemoth of dirty dishes everyone left behind.

—

My eighteenth birthday started with a long day of exams at school. I dragged my feet home. Mama greeted me at the front door, surprising me with a small marble chocolate cake and a single lit candle. I didn't have much energy but I put on a big smile and hugged her in the doorway until my arms were sore. It had been a hard year on her. My lola, back in Camarines Sur, passed away a few months prior. I caught Mama that morning with puffy red eyes.

My coming-of-age dinner was loud and the clean-up was messy. I lay in bed, counting the snores that whistled through our creaky Doonside home. Once I was sure everyone was asleep, I tiptoed out of my room with an espionage plan to sneak a midnight slice of cake. My door didn't creak like it normally did when I opened it – perhaps luck was on my side. I felt my way through the dark corridor, guided by the mismatched shelves that straddled our feature walls. My target was only a corner away. The kitchen was a warm orange, lit by the candle that sat in the centre of a full meal. I locked eyes on the flickering flame, my original plan now completely abandoned as a shudder ran all throughout my body. The pancit was cold and the smell of soy sauce wafted towards me. After what felt like hours of paralysed silence, I heard my mum's familiar fluffy tsinelas scuffing the carpet behind me. Mama hated my nightcaps. My eyes darted – scurrying to think of an excuse for why I was up. I turned to greet her but I was met with my shadow flickering on the feature walls instead. The chill in my limbs became flushes of warmth. The hairs on the back of my neck stood up. I charged into the empty corridor and my hulking silhouette, running back to my room. I slammed my door and flung myself into bed, shutting my eyes hard until I fell asleep.

The next morning, a sea of navy blue swarmed the school gates and I hastily undid my seatbelt. I didn't have a chance to fit in some last-minute studying amidst everything that was going on the night before. I fumbled with the straps as I grabbed my duffel from my feet. *Will I do okay? What if I fail? Will I be disowned?*

Just as I got out of the car, Mama handed me a deep blue rectangular container. 'For good luck,' she said. I eyed the lunchbox carefully before I stuffed it into my bag. I only just managed to fit it under my jacket. I stared forward for a moment and Mama hung her head. After what felt like a whole week of silence, it hit us both. My eyes widened as I turned to face her. She gasped and her shoulders became tense. I loosened my grip on my bag as Mama let go of her breath, placing her hand on her chest. It was the same warmth from last night and the same heaviness I felt in my chest seven times each year – but this time it stifled the chaotic thoughts that were boiling over in my head. 'She's just making sure you're okay,' Mama said, scratching the little hairs on my chin.

—

The hall doors broke open and waves of relieved graduates clambered out into the front lawn. I ran straight for the seniors' microwave and heated up my magic pancit. My friends and I converged at our regular table, completely deflated from Standard English Paper 1. Jordana, my best friend, sat quietly, her cheeks flushed red. Her warm elbows tapped mine as she slowly rubbed her temples. Grace and Eunice, my math partners, stared off into the back field. Grace held her breath as she stroked her neatly straightened hair. Eunice fumed, letting out hot air in intermittent 'hmphs'.

We all shared a gloomy glance before bursting into laughter. I placed my container next to Sheeni's, who had bagged the spot first. Hers was a burgundy square, matching the henna that swirled around her wrist. The metal table we squeezed onto resembled a potluck; boasting with sandwiches and biryani and pastries and kebabs. 'Oh my god, he messaged back!' Sheeni screamed, pushing her phone into our collective line of sight.

I laughed, bits of vermicelli falling onto my lid. 'I told you he wasn't ghosting you.'

TOURNAMENT OF THE ETHNICS

Daniel Nour

Dad's gold Rolex flies down his wrist as he slams hard onto the brakes and pushes his huge hairy brown hand into the horn. 'You bloody silly bugger! You smartie!' he shouts at an Anglo-Australian P-plater with a rat's tail. The teenager sticks his hand out the window and gives us the finger before roaring down Narellan Road.

We are Egyptian Protestants, so while it's okay to say things like 'smartie' or 'little smartie', it is never okay to say 'fucking idiot moron', which I can tell from the bulging vein in his temple is what Dad really wanted to say. He never calls me 'fucking idiot moron'. Actually, I never see him that much anyway because he wakes up at four every morning to open Mid-City Newsagency, the shop he owns on King Street near Town Hall Station. Dad usually gets home after 9pm. With me he uses nice words like 'good man' or 'good bub' and only shouts when I get my timetables wrong or my room is messy or I don't do well in a comprehension test.

It's been a long drive from leafy Menai and now I have a maghas-ache and have to do a poo. Seeing Dad upset sometimes gives me maghas but I'm also worried about today's competition at the University of Western Sydney's Campbelltown campus. I try focusing on the game of *Snake* I'm playing on Dad's Nokia 6210. The dull heavy clicks of the buttons and the jarring movements of the pixelated reptile don't distract me from the squelching in the bottom of my tummy that is spreading across my midsection. I don't want to let Dad down.

Only a few days before, he told my uncles how happy he was with me. 'Waled zaki awi! Bi etkalam kwayes bardu! – He's a very clever boy! He's a great public speaker too!' he said to Kamel, Khairy, Youssef and Nader at our house, all standing around the barbecue drinking Tooheys New. My mum and aunties were rolling vine leaves inside. All my Coptic Orthodox uncles spoke at once: 'Ah, good boy, yeah. Tournament like war. Play sport but study harder. We tell priest to say a prayer for him. Where is shish kebab?'

Nancy, my Year 6 teacher, spots us from the main seminar room as we walk into the foyer of the UWS Students' Union. Dad has a big belly but he's strong whereas I am short, weak and pudgy. I think I hear someone laughing at us but it's just a kookaburra. I wish my father looked like the White preacher dad from *7th Heaven* and that I looked like Jack Scully from *Neighbours*.

'You're quite late, Mr Nour,' Nancy says to me with a tight-lipped smile as thin as her waistline. We called Miss Powers by her first name, Nancy, because she told us she wanted to be our friend more than our teacher. Maybe that's why she was always picking on me in class, shaking her bony pale fingers at me whenever she got the chance and staring at the flab of my tummy with hungry eyes. Friends could be mean whereas teachers could not. Nancy hands me a sticker with my name on it and points to one of the side rooms down the hallway.

'Ah, we always running on Egyptian time, hey?' Dad nudges Nancy's shoulder, a twinkle in his eye. She smiles at him with her shrew face. He leaves me to her but not before saying, 'Yallah, you do excellent in this competition, bub!' Then he goes outside to take a call on his Nokia. I hear him shouting at an Indian man from Telstra.

'Please make sure that your dad puts his phone on silent,' Nancy says. She walks me toward the seminar room where my team are preparing for the debate. Along the way, she runs into another teacher and talks to her about the awesomeness of multiculturalism. Nancy, like so many others from Bangor Primary School, has never lived outside the completely Anglo-Saxon Sutherland Shire. Everyone is proud of her because this year she won a teaching award from the Department of Education.

From our classroom drill sessions with Nancy, I know there are three stages to the competition: an outdoor registration section, brainstorming time in a seminar room, and an impromptu speech prepared as a group and presented by one lucky student. 'Collaboration is the key criteria for success in Tournament of the Minds,' Nancy has told us for weeks now.

Ben Smith, our fat freckle-faced team captain, is standing in front of our group – a combination of students from all different grades who are sitting cross-legged in a circle on the green carpet. They include Ryan Esfehani, an Iranian Bahai who is always about to cry, and Lisa Cullens, who is tiny even for a ten-year-old. Kiera Müller, who is sitting closest to Ben, is the one that's been selected to deliver the speech for our group today, which is a big honour. Nancy says that Kiera is a great collaborator, but actually she's a try-hard who only gets chosen because she's cute like a von Trapp child with her blonde hair, blue eyes and straight back from years of ballet training.

On the sheet of butcher's paper, which is blue-tacked to the wall, Ben makes a big Venn diagram. Into each of the outer circles he writes 'Chinese', 'Samoan' and 'African' respectively. Then, in the middle and with huge capital letters he writes 'AUSTRALIA'. He invites us to shout out words and phrases relating to these categories.

'Fried rice!' says Ryan.

'Aboriginal people!' shouts Lisa.

'Palestine!' I say.

Ben's smile gets bigger with each word. 'This is so great guys! We're really on the right track and being sooo collaborative! Yummy!' he says like a fucking wanker. I know that none of this will make a difference because Kiera prepared her speech in advance anyway.

Still, I decide that this is as good a time as any to share my prepared notes. I tell Ben that I made a vocabulary list and pull it out of my Billabong backpack. The corners of his mouth are downturned. I read my list, saying each word loudly and clearly: 'Sikh. Melting pot. Korean hotpot. Chinese beef noodle soup. Thai curry. Green Thai curry. Panang curry. Pad Thai chicken. Jewish. Jerry Seinfeld. Commonwealth countries. Paralympic Games. Louise Sauvage. Postmodern. Lesbian. Gough Whitlam. Ernie Dingo. Inuit. Canada.' Ben is staring at me like I'm an idiot, his eyes flitting sideways to Kiera. 'What were you saying about Africa being really poor?'

The hour passes and Nancy comes in to say that it's time for us all to head to the auditorium. I stand up and walk towards the door. Ben sprints in front of me and cuts off my path. Nancy exits first, then Kiera, then Ben, then Ryan, Lisa and finally me.

Dad's shirt is darkened with sweat when he walks into the hall and his chunky Nokia phone is protruding from his pocket. He moves his large body through the pews to get to his chair as his phone hits some of the White mums on the backs of their heads. Their mouths stretch into tight smiles but they're otherwise perfectly still. His ringtone is called 'The Buffoon' and usually brings grocery requests from Mum or payment reminders from Coca-Cola Amatil. Now, the phone sits dormant in his pocket like an Israeli landmine in the Sinai.

We are all sitting down in the semi-circle shaped auditorium. There is a buzzing in my ears that has nothing to do with the whir of the air-conditioning. We all really want to win and Kiera is up first. 'Multiculturalism is a concept that Australia invented to stop racism,' she begins, pausing after this opening line to make prolonged, unnerving eye contact with everyone in the front row. 'There are many ways that Australia is a multicultural country,' she returns to her text, staring at the cue cards. 'Firstly, our food is diverse: on a weekday in the Shire where I live, you can enjoy…' and at this point, she spreads her hand out theatrically, motioning for her guests to enjoy an invisible banquet, 'Lebanese, Greek, Turkish and modern Australian cuisine, which is a mix of Thai food with more normal foods like steak and broccoli.'

It starts as a soft echo at first but then grows louder and louder, the sound of 'The Buffoon' reverberating through the room: *Da-da da dum dum dum*. Dad sits relaxed, smiling inexplicably in his chair. My world is ending.

I stare at him, trying to communicate telepathically. These White ladies already hate me, so what must they think of me and my big hairy explosive dad now? The ringing stops quickly, just in time for Kiera to begin her second point – something about the importance of different races all getting along and how the Wik decision solved the problem of Aboriginal Land Rights forever.

Then the ringing starts again. It's louder this time and one of the parents, a mousy blonde woman in tights and a cardigan, turns her head and stares at Dad. My legs feel like lead. I will the floor to open up and swallow me like a sinkhole did for one of my uncle's best friends in the Six-Day War.

'Racism is bad, but unity is—' Kiera tries to continue.

Da-da da dum dum dum da-da da da dum…

Now Dad also starts looking around for the culprit, as though he's wondering why this fool isn't turning their phone off.

Finally the mousy blonde snaps, twisting her little head quickly to the side, the edges of her bob bouncing lightly. 'Turn it off! My goodness!' she hisses at him. She turns back to her friend and they both raise their eyebrows in disbelief.

Iranian Ryan, who, with his asymmetric bowl cut and vacant cow eyes, has the jumpy manner of a prey animal, starts crying. 'Ryan, we'll lose points if you look sad,' Ben whispers angrily, even redder in the face than usual.

Incredibly, Dad's phone is still ringing. What kind of a person calls a man for this long? My father's chaotic search through the sea of baggy polyester that is his trouser leg lasts for an eternity. He is Aladdin trawling through a cave of trinkets for his precious lamp.

'Allo? Yeah, Fareed Nour speaking!' Dad shouts, rising to his feet and stomping out with all the noise and drama of an M1 Abrams Tank. The seminar room door slams behind him.

Ryan, who is now crying and hiccupping at the same time, asks me if the man with the phone is my dad. I say, 'I don't know that guy.'

Suddenly, an ear-splitting screech erupts from the auditorium speakers. Nancy rushes to the microphone, nudging Kiera aside and directing everyone to make for the car park in a calm single file line. We arrive at the emergency meeting point. Five minutes later, Nancy is nervously chatting with the other teachers while tiny Lisa tells me that her dad also had to evacuate his construction site in Penrith once because a builder started a fire by throwing his cigarette into a rubbish pile.

At last, Nancy comes over to our team and explains that we'll receive the verdict via email once the other schools present their speeches at a centre in Homebush and that we should all go home. Dad is still on his phone near the bottle brush plants, too angry at Telstra to notice that we have an emergency situation.

As we drive past the rolling green hills of Sydney's South West, he asks me, 'Why did that girl get to speak and you not? Is that girl better than you?' I cry a little that night, feelings of shame and failure and horniness all swirling around my hormonally pudgy and pimply twelve-year-old body.

The next morning, I come downstairs to find breakfast – two cheese and Vegemite toasties and a cup of milky tea – laid out on the kitchen bench. Mum is washing dishes and Dad is drinking coffee from a giant mug that says: *DAD!* He is never usually home this late in the morning. He has taken the day off to drive me to school.

The car ride over is silent. Have I done something to disappoint him? Is he angry about Kiera's speech?

We park and he swishes in his polyester trousers, back straight and belly out, into the deputy principal's office. I sit in the office hallway, tapping my feet against the carpeted floor. *Please Lord Jesus, don't let him embarrass me again.* Shame, hot and strong, rises in my cheeks. I had disappointed my teacher – why else would she look at me with those cold eyes that told me I didn't belong in her classroom? I had betrayed my father too, ashamed of him and his Arab look.

Dad's gravelly voice cuts through my sad daydreams. 'I don't bloody care what you say about Nancy. She is a racist woman and she is ignoring my son on purpose.' The two chubby White ladies who run the school office look at each other nervously and continue working as though nothing is happening. 'That's wrong, you can't ignore some students and let others have a chance!' I hear Dad say, his scream bursting out of Mr Miller's office and down the corridor. 'She hates my son!'

Kyle and Chris, also in Year 6 but sportier than me, run in to get some band aids. They hear the shouting and throw me a series of cocky glances before running out again. Dad trudges out of the office angrily. I have to run to keep up with his big strides, up over the asphalt basketball court and out into the car park.

We go straight to Red Rooster. I ask for two crunchy rolls with roast chicken and extra gravy. The cashier stares at my pudgy body with its flabby rolls of tummy fat. When I walk out with the two sandwich bags, Dad sees my sad eyes and chunky frame. He takes me by the hand and says, 'You should never feel embarrassed about who you are, habibi.'

We eat our rolls in silence on a park bench near the restaurant. 'The Buffoon' starts ringing on my dad's Nokia. He is shouting down the phone at his landlord about why he's charging a rort deal on the rental payments. 'Don't be a bloody smartie!'

SUPERBROW

Monikka Eliah

Burnt orange foundation pooled at the bottom of an empty Homebrand Neapolitan ice cream container. I was the first actor to have my face painted. I sat on a flakey faux leather stool in the corner of the main hall at PCYC Cabramatta. The King and Anna practised 'It's a Puzzlement' to music blaring from a small silver Sony stereo and the rest of the cast stood against the four walls watching. Not that there was much to see. I should have been Anna. The director, a teapot-shaped woman with too much chin and not enough eyebrow, had told me I didn't get the part because I was too young. But I knew it was because Anna was to be played by a Mary Poppins-type and I was more Omar Sharif from *Lawrence of Arabia*. The King's voice bounced from his belly like Santa Claus, 'Shall I join with other nations in alliance?' The music skipped every time he was directed to stamp his bare foot against the wooden floor panels. It reminded me of my little sister pounding her feet when she wanted a strawberry Roll-up.

The make-up artist forced bubbles to froth to the surface of the container each time she dipped a white wedged sponge into it. Her hair was tied in a ponytail, the ends the colour and texture of pork crackling. Her nose was pink and pinched at the tip like Cindy Lou Who. I had heard about the production four months ago when my ESL teacher, Mrs Manska, had read the audition notice aloud to us, her yellow nails digging into a clipping from *The Fairfield Champion*. Gathered around a Windows 98 in her small office, filled with stacks of paper and dirty dishes, Mrs Manska leaned over my shoulder. Her sour coffee breath fanned my left cheek as we looked on the internet for free monologues. The sunlight streaming through the dirt-stained window had cast green shadows across the room. After forty minutes of browsing, I found one I liked about a dead grandma and an aspiring actress. My grandma was still alive but the part about the aspiring actress was soul-baring. It mentioned something called 'valet stubs' that I assumed meant a studded silk pillow. It sounded dramatic and glamorous. The monologue ended with the character crying. I practised sticking my bottom lip out far enough to tremble and staring into the distance unblinking until my eyes watered. Mrs Manska told me I was sensational.

Cindy Lou swiped the soaked sponge across my cheeks, chin and forehead. The mixture felt cold against my skin. It smelt like the dried and crushed roses Mama put in a bowl on the edge of our bathtub at home. Some of the foundation dribbled down my neck and I had to pull my collar away from my chest to stop it from staining. The shirt was a gift from my aunt in America. White polyester blend and decorated with diamantes. It was the fanciest thing I owned. I wore it desperately hoping someone would ask me where it was from. They never did.

Cindy Lou pulled my chin to tilt my head back, causing my eyes to line up with her chest. Her boobies were smaller than Mama's but she wore a magenta bra I'd never seen in my mother's drawer of black and beige. I didn't have a drawer like that yet. I kept my two cotton crop tops folded beside my white school socks. I shut my eyes quickly and stayed as still as possible only to have her click her tongue, hold my chin and move my head in a new direction. Her movements were quick and her plastic French-tips dug into my skin as though she was angry with my face. I tried to smile at her but she tapped a finger on my nose and told me to close my mouth. Then she started to blend the colour with dabbing motions across my lips.

'So, how old are you?' She looked like a Who, but she sounded like the phlegm traps that bought cigarettes from the Food For Less counter in Fairfield Heights. I remembered her order to keep my mouth shut and was unsure of what to do. 'Hey... can you speak English?' I nodded and felt her pinch my chin again to keep my head still. 'How old are you?'

'Twelve,' I squeaked.

She hummed as she slipped the skinny edge of the sponge between the folds in my right ear. I tried to yank myself away and felt her tug on my earlobe. 'Stay still or you'll be patchy.'

I didn't want to be patchy, I wanted to be beautiful. I hadn't had my make-up done before. There were pictures of me as a child in Jordan wearing red lipstick my mama had smudged across my mouth and I had once snuck into her room to swipe crushed apricot blush on my cheeks, but to sit on a stool and have a professional paint my face was something else entirely. Desperate to look my best, I let Cindy Lou continue to colour the inside of my ears, then my jaw, chin and neck. Compared with the pimply faces of my peers, my skin would stand out as smooth and clear as a hard-boiled egg in a bowl of oats.

I shifted in the stool and looked over at Aberto, the hottie with a body and the full lips I dreamed of kissing. He was standing with Amber, a dancer. They were talking and laughing, her freckled cheeks flushed pink. I watched her run her fingers through the dark curly hair on his calf and felt my ears heat up. *Oh, that I were a dead skin cell upon that leg!* The King stomped his foot again and forced the CD to stop. In the moment of quiet, I overhead Amber telling Aberto his legs were too hairy. *They aren't too hairy for me! Oh Aberto, why are you wasting your time with Amber, can't you see that I am your soulmate?* Three months of rehearsal and he was no closer to being my boyfriend. How many times did I have to pretend to fall over in front of him? My knees couldn't take it! I tried to catch his eyes now. I'd seen in the movies how a look from across a room could be the beginning of a romance. I could be the Rose to his Leonardo DiCaprio. What was the character's name? Tom? John?

'Shut your eyes,' Cindy Lou instructed. I begrudgingly obeyed, felt something sharp trace across my eyebrows. I wasn't allowed to pluck them but I snuck my mother's tweezers into the bathroom once a month to pull out the two hairs that grew just above my nose. Monobrows were fugly. A monobrow, a mole and fat lips, that's how everyone defaced the photographs in our high school textbooks. Next I felt something wet across my lash line. *Eyeliner, yes! My eyes will look just like Haifa Wehbe's.* Cindy Lou took a deep breath and blew against my eyelids. It smelt like cheese. A sharp and aged cheddar. I ignored the scent and tried to imagine what Aberto's breath would be like. Probably milky and sweet like Chobani yoghurt and M&M's. I'd never kissed a boy before but how hard could it be? You just licked your lips moist with saliva and then pushed them out like a blowfish. I'd practised in the mirror, pursing my lips out until they started to hurt.

Cindy Lou tapped me on the shoulder to get my attention. 'Your face is done.'

'Really? How do I look?'

'Good, I s'pose.'

Good? She said I look good! Wow. I smiled at her and slid off the chair, walking over to Aberto and Amber with my chin in the air and my hands on my hips.

'Sup guys.' I tried to sound sultry and confident like Marissa from *The O.C.*, a show that I wasn't allowed to watch but had gathered all of the important parts from the ads on Channel Ten. I stood with one foot out, my toes pointed in Aberto's direction. *Dolly* magazine had taught me all about body language. Aberto's brain would subconsciously pick this up as a signal of my attraction and interest. He looked over at me and smiled. I felt my palms start to sweat and fluttered my eyelashes at him. *That's right, notice my eyeliner.*

'So, like, what are you up to?' I pretended to be unaffected by his attention and casually swiped a strand of hair behind my ear, but the sweat made my fingers sticky. *Does he like the make-up or does he think I look better without it? Will he whisper to me that I'm a natural beauty that doesn't need make-up to look good?*

'I was just telling Aberto he needs to shave his legs. Look at them!' Amber pointed and I followed her finger to Aberto's tanned calves. I wanted to bite them and get his curls caught in my teeth.

'Oh my god, yeah gross,' I lied.

Amber giggled like a small bird and I echoed her, trying to match the tone and volume of her laugh.

The King and Anna finished their practise and the director waggled her chin as she shouted out my character's name. 'Tuptim! We're doing "Small House of Uncle Thomas" now.' Sure, I wasn't Anna but as the King's mistress, Tuptim was an equally important role. I grabbed a plastic chair and walked over to the stage-outline taped on the floor. I took a seat just right of centre and a cluster of kids kneeled around my feet. I put my arms up in front of me pretending to hold a piece of parchment and the music on the stereo begun. *Anna, eat your heart out.*

The introduction was sung by everyone on stage: 'Small house of Uncle Thomas. Small house of Uncle Thomas. Written by a woman, Harriet Beecher Stowe.' The 'wa' on 'Stowe' was always exaggerated; it hurled through the air like a frisbee.

After a pause, I spoke. 'House is in Kingdom of Kentucky. Ruled by most wicked king in all America, Simon of Legree.'

The director stopped the music. 'No, we talked about this.' She crouched down to face me and I lowered my arms. Her thin eyebrows looked like squished ants up close. She repeated the line I had just spoken, breaking each word into syllables and tightening the vowels so that 'house' sounded like 'hows' and 'kentucky' sounded like 'kintuckee'. The phrasing was splintered like a tree branch that had been cut by a blunt knife. I nodded my head, but when I opened my mouth to mimic her, I found I was fighting myself. I spent my first four years in Australia learning to drop Rs for Ys, softening Ts in the middle of a word and dropping Gs at the end of words. Wiya. Playa. Saderday. Gowin. Geddin. If I hadn't spoken perfect 'Astrayan' in the audition, I would have never gotten the part.

The kneeling kids around me looked up, waiting. The director frowned, her ant eyebrows kissing in the middle. 'If you want to be a professional actor, you need to take this seriously.' Of course, I wanted to be a professional actor! I imagined myself in the *Neighbours* opening theme, pretending to laugh as my bottle blonde hair billowed behind me.

I stiffened my arms in front of me and the director stepped back to turn the stereo on. 'Hows is in King-dom of Kin-tuck-ee. Ruled by most wick-ed king in all Am-er-ica, Si-mon of Le-gree.' I continued the choppy phrasing for the rest of the song. When it was over, my mouth felt dry and the muscles in my forearms ached. I stood from the chair and walked back towards the wall where Aberto was watching.

'You remember so many lines.'

His compliment made my abdominal muscles tense. 'Thanks.'

I wanted to say more but I felt less confident with Amber absent. I wished we could practise Act Two: Scene Four. Aberto and another actor named Danny played guards who had found my character trying to escape. I was carried in their arms and thrown down on the ground. It was too rough and my legs hurt but my heart always beat faster and harder for all of those twelve seconds – Aberto's hands touching my bicep. Then the King would threaten to whip me and I would have to cling to Anna's giant hoop skirt and beg. Beg her to stop the barbaric King from hurting me. 'Mrs Anna, Mrs Anna. Do not let them beat me. Do not let them.' Finally, my character would be carried off to the dungeon by Aberto and Danny, never to be seen again. A scene later, the whole cast had to join hands and sing 'Getting to Know You'. I never understood how Mrs Anna could smile and sing while I, Tuptim, was rotting in the dungeon.

I felt Aberto staring at my face. *Is he drawn to my body language? What if he tries to kiss me?* My upper lip started to sweat. He probably saw me with the make-up and found me utterly irresistible. I didn't blame him. *This must be what supermodels feel like.* My hands started to shake. It was probably my souped-up hormones zipping around. I read about what happens when boys and girls are alone in P.E. *I'm not ready to have a baby!*

'Are you okay?'

I turned away from Aberto and sprinted to the bathroom. I heard him call after me and I picked up speed. Two hands in front, I pushed the toilet door open. Inside, three side-by-side mirrors reflected my image. 'Oh god!'

My face floated like a rusty orange blister against the pale skin of my chest and shoulders, a freshly roasted piece of tandoori tikka on flatbread; my eyes had been extended on either corner with thick black lines so they stretched out across each cheek; and my eyebrows, two rectangles, jutted out diagonally towards my hairline. *I don't look beautiful, I look angry*. Every feature was exaggerated just like a school photo someone had drawn over in permanent marker. No one on *Neighbours* would ever have looked like this! I stepped towards the sink and turned the tap on, trying to wash away the eyebrows but they smudged and melted into one superbrow. Monobrows were fugly. I was fugly. I turned off the tap and felt my cheeks heating and my throat clogging. I thought about how closely I had stood beside Aberto, batting my eyelashes. *Why would Cindy Lou do this?* The heat in my cheeks shimmied across my face and down my neck. I wasn't embarrassed anymore, I was furious. I turned back towards the toilet door and pushed it open, hard enough to hear it slam against the wall. I ran back to the main hall, cut across the actors rehearsing and went straight to Cindy Lou and her make-up station. 'You fucking Grinch! You call yourself a make-up artist? I look nothing like Haifa Wehbe!'

LOOKING CLASSY, WHAT ARE YOU?

Shirley Le

Sitting on a silver bench inside Macquarie Uni Station, I swipe right on twenty-five-year-old Jason from Marrickville as soon as his solid Viet head pops up on my phone. Broad chest underneath a grey crew neck sweater. Skin the colour of freshly split sapôchê. I hope he smells like sapôchê too – brown sugar melting into a slice of cucumber. I run a finger across the screen, wondering how it'd feel to stroke his thick straight eyebrows and heart-shaped lips.

My parents told me that Marrickville was where all the North Viets live. I've never met a Viet from the Inner West. Would they be more hip and woke than the Viets in Bankstown or Cabra? After the war ended on 30 April 1975, eighty thousand Viets came to Australia and most of them were from South Vietnam, including my parents. That day, my dad sat near the front door of his house clutching a handgun. If the Viet Cong came knocking, he'd shoot himself in the head because he'd rather die than be hassled by commies. My mother was home too but she was less worried. Most of her neighbours revealed themselves to be communists all along by hanging up red flags and celebrating. She'd have to try and join the party if she wanted to keep her job as a chemistry teacher.

I'm not despo enough to start the convo with Jason but as soon as we match, I upload a new pic that I took last week while I waited for Tammy in Windows Café. It's a selfie of me with falsies on and my straightened hair pushed over one shoulder. The pink sweater I wear in the photo is more librarian than ABG, but the fabric is tight enough to show the curve of my left boob. That day I'd worn one of the perfumes that Tammy bought me for my twentieth birthday – Marc Jacobs Daisy, which smelled like flowers dipped in vodka.

Jason takes the bait. *Looking classy, what are you?* is his opening line. Is he under the impression that I am one of those lily-skinned and stick-thin K-pop stars? IRL I'm closer to the stocky freshies working in the back kitchen of phở restaurants.

Viet, I reply.

I'm Viet too, he says. *Thought you were Korean or Japanese tho.*

I tuck my hands into the sleeves of my sweater and keep on typing. *Was that what you were hoping for?*

Nah. A pretty girl's a pretty girl. LGBT?

I'm straight, I tell him.

Nah silly. Let's get bubble tea 😜

How did he have the confidence to pull off such a crap line? Maybe he had a deep smoothfm voice. My mum said that North Viets have miệng dẻo – stretchy and flexible mouths that can embellish, exaggerate and manipulate. According to her, that's how they sold the communist fantasy to the rest of Việt Nam.

I leave Jason hanging on *read* while I fact-check what he's told me. LinkedIn provides some clues. *Jason Truong. Accountant at KPMG. Studied at UNSW and was President of VSA throughout his commerce accounting degree. Graduated from Ruse class of '05.*

Facebook reveals much much more about his early twenties: during his presidency of the Vietnamese Students' Association, he organised many a nem nướng bbq and most notably, a cruise themed Tropical Trubble. There, he wore one of those tank tops with the armholes drooping low enough to show off the muscles along his ribcage. They remind me of the pork ribs from Pizza Hut, tanned and glistening. A nón lá finished off the look. Defqon.1 meets the jungle. Fellow Viets in the comments wrote, *10/10 would smash*, and a random White guy – there were always one or two in VSA who got called 'Honorary Viets' – chimed in with, *Whatta sick cunt.*

I can tell from the pics that Jason is a typical Viet bro flashing his muscles and getting digits off the hottest chicks at Bamboo on Saturday nights. For sure he's a shithead, but if Jason and I get together I'd be reaching and he'd be settling. I don't have as many friends as him, am not as fit as him and don't earn as much as he does. We aren't really xứng đôi but neither are many other Vietnamese couples around me, particularly the first-generation of Vietnamese-Australians.

Take my Ba and Mẹ for example. In Vietnam, they were relatively xứng đôi – an engineer and a chemistry teacher. But when they came to Australia, my mother worked as a mail officer at Australia Post earning an annual salary of $30,000.00 a year for twenty years straight. My father returned to university to reobtain his engineering qualifications. During the day, my mother worked and my father studied. In the evenings, they sewed cushion covers in the garage to make more money. Eventually, my dad got a job as an engineer and his salary reached $150,000.00.

On Sunday mornings, Dad gave my mother her weekly allowance. They had a fight once over how much money they should be sending to our relatives in Vietnam. Mum complained about her parents receiving less than Dad's. My dad said that his side of the family was bigger. He drove off in the Honda by himself and she didn't receive her allowance for the whole day. It reminded my mother who was boss in the house and who she depended on.

When my father came home in the evening, Mum asked me, 'Hỏi Ba cho con ăn Tim Tam – Ask Dad if you can have Tim Tams.' I found Ba in the backyard where he was squatting at the dog bowl and scooping out food for Benny. I asked him for Tim Tams. My dad knew how much I loved them and they were usually a treat for getting one hundred percent in spelling tests. 'Okay, Ba cho tiềng Mẹ mua,' he replied. He returned into the house and gave Mum the money for the week.

I flick over Jason's profile on Facebook again and notice the girls that he poses with in photos. They all have dáng đẹp whereas I have a thick waist and muscular legs. I might not even make it to a second date with Jason. From his Facebook pics, it looks like he just wants girls who are skinny with big boobs. What would Tammy do? This wouldn't be an issue for her. She's currently juggling three men who are all richer and smarter than her. I want to know the secrets to her success.

I agree to Jason's offer for a bubble tea and decide to ask Tammy for tips beforehand...

—

Central Station on a sunny Saturday morning is a wet dream for Tourism Australia. Posh East Asians everywhere following their tour guides to the Sydney Opera House. The ones in front of me, slamming their Chanel bags into the train barricades, are Korean.

One umma takes off her green visor and shoos at the seagulls who are trying to pull off a heist for her hot chips. The seagulls close in on her. Umma shrieks. The gulls back off and target her husband instead, two of them yanking his cheeseburger clean from his fingertips. Oppa roars and shakes his fist at the blue Sydney sky, Omega watch gleaming.

This intense incident is like the scenes in the Korean dramas that I watch at home with my parents. The one that we're hooked on right now is called *My Lovely Girl* and it has a typical K-drama storyline where a mega rich company CEO falls for an innocent and ditzy young girl.

'Dăng minh quá. Thằng Nam Hàng ngon qúa,' Ba clicked his tongue as the CEO stood at a window and surveyed the rest of Seoul, a network of skyscrapers and roads glowering blue and yellow. 'So civilised. Those South Koreans are doing so damn well.'

'Nếu cọng sãn không chiếm miềng Nam, giơ này mình củng như vậy,' Mum said. 'If the communists hadn't invaded South Vietnam, we would be like them by now.'

I weave through the crazy rich Asians at Central Station, Converse sneakers screeching along linoleum. Maybe these weren't the best shoes to impress a hot date. Beforehand, Tammy had told me to go with a pair of Rubi wedges but shit, I couldn't walk a metre in those without rolling an ankle. Either way, I am running ten minutes late for my date with Jason.

At 12:20pm, I skid through the front door of Song Tea in Chinatown, knocking over a stuffed alpaca that is stationed next to a sandwich board listing the store's drinks. I catch the alpaca before it crashes to the floor. Its body feels hard and hollow despite being covered in wooly curls. A K-pop ballad is playing in the background and for a moment I imagine myself as the bumbling and ditzy girl in a K-drama; a Korean me who is about to meet the love of her life. Korean me has a straight fringe, too much blush on her cheeks and large tortoise shell glasses that make her eyes bug out from the rest of her face. She wears shirts with Peter Pan collars and walks through life pigeon-toed. She crashes her baby pink bike into the hood of a BMW on the backseat of which a rock-jawed CEO is sitting. He demands that she pay for the damages to his vehicle by working for free as an intern in his company for the next year. Miraculously, Korean me agrees to the deal.

'Tinder girl?' A voice so deep that the soundwaves weave themselves into my skull is calling my name. The tips of my ears tingle. I stand the alpaca upright and look up at Jason – a Viet shaped like a polar bear. Shoulder-boulders fill out the sleeves of his Uniqlo flannel shirt, thighs strain the seams of his chinos too. I puff my stomach out under my sundress and straighten up my posture. I'm relieved. Even if I get fat, he'd still be bigger than me.

We say hi and when he leans in for a hug, I smell Dove pomegranate bodywash on his neck. His sapôchê hands feel cool against my bare shoulders and there are goosebumps left behind when he lifts his fingers off my skin. I smooth my sweaty palms on the skirt of my dress. Yellow cotton sticks to my hands and I take to tucking my hair behind my ears.

'Wanna bubble tea?' Jason bends down a couple of centimetres, trying to look me in the eye.

I avoid his gaze. 'I'll order my own thanks.' I fumble in my purse for my wallet and stand in the queue.

'Right.' He stands beside me. He must think I'm frigid but I want to show Jason that I won't be handing myself over to him like a chip for a seagull. Afterall, I had received advice from a professional: Tammy. She had three words for me. 'Don't. Get. Dickmatised.' Dickmatisation is when you put a guy on a pedestal and let him have the upper hand. Fuckbois, men who fuck you and leave you, are experts at dickmatisation.

I order a lychee tea with bubbles and shake the plastic cup before setting it on the table. Jason orders a regular milk tea with bubbles too. What a basic bitch. Tammy told me that signs like this are an indication that a guy is 'boring in bed'. I've never had sex so I don't know what that really means. We sit opposite each other near the front of the store at a round table next to the alpaca. Its eyes are made of black glass pebbles with the iridescence of petrol. The alpaca leans forward, hissing, 'Do not get dickmatised!' I clutch the straw in my fist and punch it through the plastic film covering the cup. Jason rips the plastic halfway – maybe the rest of the plastic is a scoop to catch his two brain cells if they fall out – and slides the straw into the cup. I watch as he gently holds the straw in place with fingers as thick as churros. His heart-shaped lips close around the top of the straw and milky liquid shoots up the plastic. They're bigger than I expected and I lick my own lips, hoping that the moisture will hide the dry bits poking out of the crevices.

'You got full sugar?' He cocks his left pinky in my direction while the rest of his fingers grip his drink.

Don't get dickmatised. 'Yeh, why not?'

'You're a small girl, not as small as my sister though,' he replies.

I suck in my gut. 'So, you want a girl as skinny as your sister?'

'No, I'd prefer a girl smaller than me though. I swear that's what most guys want.'

I don't have a response for him. I can't even breathe properly right now. I've sucked in my gut so far that it feels like it's sticking to my spine. I went on my first diet when I was twelve. I'd gotten braces and it was painful to chew. Each day, the only food I ate was a bowl of congee for dinner. My mouth was full of ulcers and my hair fell out in clumps but my stomach was flat and I had a thigh gap. Then I blacked out on the train to school one morning. I'd slept in and caught the 10:30am train from Bankstown to Central. There was no one else in the carriage. I woke up back in Bankstown, after the locomotive had taken a full circle around the city. That's when I realised I had taken my diet too far and swung the other way, eating a whole box of Cornettos straight after school. These days I go through phases: binging and purging, waxing and waning. In the last three months, I've started eating breakfast and dinner again.

'I'm talking shit. You make me nervous,' Jason says quickly. He reaches out and hooks the tip of his index finger around the tip of my index finger, which is resting on my cup of bubble tea. I catch his finger and turn it over so that the underside is facing me. It's like that scene in *E.T.* where the alien wants to phone home. Jason smiles. A constellation of four moles trailing down his left cheek shifts upwards. His teeth are like mine and any other kid who had braces: white and straight.

Over the counter, the machines pumping out different flavours of milk tea continue whirring and the smell of brown sugar suspends me in a vat of syrup. The K-pop ballad has reached a crescendo, male voice ringing. What does the lead girl in a K-drama do when the CEO negs her? She puffs and pouts her cherry lips. The CEO smirks and rolls his eyes. They engage with each other in a tedious courtship but in the end, she steers him from his arsehole ways, shows him how to be tender and how to love. He teaches her that true love is putting up with his bullshit no matter what.

Jason slurps the rest of his tea and chews on the tapioca bubbles – smacks them between his teeth the same way the uncles in Bankstown do when they take a sip of good coffee, 'Ahhh đã quá.' When he finishes, he holds up the empty plastic cup for me to see. His eyes shine like longan seeds. I can tell that he shows his mother his empty bowl when she asks him, 'Ăn cơm xong chưa?' He's waiting for me to praise him like his mother but I look down at my own cup and suck the last two bubbles up the straw and swallow them whole. I show him my empty cup.

'Ruột để ngoài da,' I tell him, 'Guts on your skin.' My parents say this when someone is revealing too much about themselves.

'Cái gì? I've never heard of that before,' he replies. He pronounces gì like zee, just like Solicitor Dung in Bankstown, the only North Vietnamese person I know in South West Sydney. Behind his back, my parents mock his accent by calling him 'Luật sư Dzzzunggg', which means 'Lawyer Dung'.

I like the feeling of knowing something that Jason doesn't. The way his puffy lips droop when I don't praise him for the tiniest shit is also cute. If we end up together, it won't be too hard to keep him in check. All I need to do is starve him in the right ways. It would be thrilling to control a guy who is hotter, richer and bigger than me. I hear Tammy's voice in my head. *Don't get dickmatised and everything will be fine.*

FUSI

Kabien Parker

HYPO

One time, I remember having to run into the shops to buy some groceries for the dinner. The way I had to pay for it was by my mum's credit card. I felt pretty embarrassed carrying something that I knew wasn't even mine. Also being an annoying little hypo seven-year-old alone in the shops carrying a credit card.

I walked up to the counter to buy my items. I remember the cashier had a face like she just smelled the dog poo after picking it up off of the floor. When I was younger, I was darker, so now I see why she made the weird face while doing my shopping. She just threw the items in the bag, not even worrying about cracking them eggs and bruising them fruits. Since I was younger and not too familiar with similar events like this one, I didn't know what to do; I just stood there watching.

When the cashier finished, I walked back out to the car, drove home. I remember Mum screaming at me, 'Oi, kid, what happened to the eggs? And why are the fruits all bruised up? Bloody useless!'

BASH ME

One time at dinner, there was one more piece of chicken left. Me and my brother fought for it for the next few minutes. After those few minutes, it broke into an argument.

'You're fat bro, the youngest shouldn't be eating as much as the oldest.'

'Look at yourself before calling me fat!'

'Fatty, go away before I actually bash you.'

'As if you can even bash me.'

Then my mum came into the room and we both got a fusi.

BIKER KIDS

One time at the park, I was sitting on the swing, and these bunch of Year 6 little biker kids were acting all cool playing their OneFour music, swearing and stuff. One of them thought I was a friend of theirs and said, 'Tom, wassup my n****.'

BLOODY FALI'I

ring ring

'Oi hurry up and get the phone!'
'Why don't you, you're right there m8!'
'I'm the oldest, Mum said you have to listen to the oldest you fiapoko, now go get the phone!'
'Fine fine chill.'
'That's right.'
'Sook.'
'What m8?'
'Nothing nothing nothing...'
'Smh that's right.'
'Bloody fali'i kid.'

HUGE

some tongan stereotypes:
they like horses
really really loud
we both are huge

PALANGI

Chris Tupouniua

A WANNABE ISLANDER

I remember one day in 2019, I went to my primary school and these palangi boys and girls called me plastic, which is pretty much when you're a wannabe Islander. I remember that during the day I was cut and angry because I was being judged by White people who think they know what a Tongan really is when they probably haven't ever met a real Islander. After that, I went back to play handball with my friends. I haven't felt any worse than being called a wannabe of my own culture. I've also been called plastic by other Islanders. I've also heard people thinking I was dumb and mean just because I was Islander. I was thinking back ago to when I lived in Tonga, when life was easy and chill, but I guess this is life now.

THE 676

'What nash are you guys?'
'Me & him are from Tonga.'
'As in, the 676 Tonga?'
'Yeah.'
'Are you half?'
'Nah.'
'Where are youse from?'
'I'm from Hofoa.'
'What about you?'
'I'm from Popua.'
'Actualls?'
'Yea, what about you?'
'I'm from Tofoa.'
'Near the hospital?'
'Yea bruv.'
'Ok laterz toks.'
'Lo tau toki sio.'
'Lo.'

GHEEBAH IN THE OFFICE KITCHEN

Ferdous Bahar

'Poor thing. The way her hajeeb sticks out in the firm photo.' Vanessa's phlegmy voice cuts through the hum of beeping printers and rustling contracts in our open plan office. I would have been less surprised if she had slapped me across the face. The tips of my ears burn underneath my hijab and the fabric itches on each point of my face and neck that it touches. A group of senior lawyers walk out of a meeting across the room. I am grateful that they are too far away to see the smoke coming out of my ears. 'Everyone's in blacks and greys and then this blob of maroon.' Her lunch companion murmurs something in response under soft drink cans cracking open and laughter like rattling cutlery. 'Love her to bits but how long do you reckon she's going to last?' Vanessa slurps loudly as she downs her drink. 'One of the seniors was giving her shit about her work last week, did you know?' Vanessa lowers her voice until she is inaudible.

Warm saliva gathers at the back of my throat. Am I going to throw up? *Astaghfirullah: I seek forgiveness in God.* The phrase spills out of me when I am in the presence of something shameful or disgusting

– the same phrase my parents use when talking about corrupt politicians in Dhaka and Pauline Hanson in Australia.

Astaghfirullah, astaghfirullah, astaghfirullah, astaghfirullah, astaghfirullah, astaghfirullah, astaghfirullah, astaghfirullah, astaghfirullah, astaghfirullah, astaghfirullah, astaghfirullah, astaghfirullah, astaghfirullah, astaghfirullah, astaghfirullah.

Vanessa and I have been best friends since starting in Frank Morris Law's insolvency team as junior lawyers six months ago. On our first day in the team, one of the senior executives proposed a drinks celebration to welcome the new junior lawyers. I opened my mouth to ask about non-alcoholic drinks but Vanessa, with a glance in my direction, beat me to it. 'Wouldn't a coffee celebration be a little more inclusive?' She flashed her straight white teeth as the other junior lawyers fidgeted uncomfortably around us.

The senior executive's wrinkly smile turned into a frown, 'Yes... I guess not everyone enjoys a free wine.' His tongue slipped out of his mouth as he laughed.

'Yes, and some people don't drink at all! Shock horror,' she grinned back at the senior executive, batting her brown eyelashes at him until he twisted his mouth into a smile. From that moment, alcoholic drink events were few and far between at the firm.

As Vanessa continues stabbing my back in the office kitchen, I remember the khutbahs, Friday sermons, about gheebah that our local imam shared over the crackly microphones at Minto Mosque. Soft green and orange fabric curling between my toes as Mum brushed her fingertips across my hand, whispering at me to stop drawing patterns in the carpet and listen. So many of the sermons were about gheebah: gossiping and backbiting. Any Muslim will tell you that gheebah is a major sin. It's up there with adultery and murder. The act of speaking ill of someone behind their back is like eating the flesh of your dead brother. Right now, Vanessa is having a feast.

My breath splinters in my throat like ilish bones as I hear scraping chairs in the kitchen. Vanessa is going to walk past my desk any minute. I whisper a final 'astaghfirullah' as her chunky high heels clop across the floorboards and towards my desk.

'Hey,' she says, smiling and waving at me like she hasn't just consumed a dead body in the kitchen. 'Missed you at lunch today! Let's grab some tomorrow.' She grins, showing me more of her teeth. I imagine red-stained gums and spots of dried blood between her lips and chin. The stench of a corpse fills the space between our bodies. How shameless to be standing there without a crease of remorse on her face.

My nostrils flare and every line in my face twists with disgust as I glare into Vanessa's grey-green eyes. The audacity of this absolute rat. Her high-heel makes a single 'clop' as she takes a half-step back. 'Vanessa,' I breathe out, my voice warming my lips. 'You've forgotten how close my desk is to the kitchen.'

Her mouth hangs open in a silent gasp. Her teeth are stained with Coke and biscuit crumbs, the tips of her canines disappearing and reappearing as she opens and closes her mouth. Her eyes glance all over my face and then around the office, as if one of our colleagues will jump in and save her from our conversation.

'What you said about me...' I say the words slowly, like I would to a toddler. Her smooth olive-tone forehead crumples with skinny lines. 'It was probably an accident but... jeez.' I rub my index finger on my chin. This is so awkward. Vanessa raises her hands to her cheeks. *Oh my God, is she going to cry?* 'Look, I'm late for prayer.' I turn and pick up the prayer mat I keep on the side of my desk with shaking fingers. I'm still angry. Maybe dhuhr prayer will calm me down.

'Bestie...' The rat has found her voice. I turn to look at her and notice her eyes are all watery. She really is about to cry.

'Not interested,' I cut her off, pressing my blue and gold prayer mat to my chest as I take a step away, distancing myself from her stained teeth and wet eyeballs. 'I'm going to pray now. I hope you had a good gheebah.'

Her eyes light up. Does she think this is an olive branch? I'm so angry I've crumpled a corner of my prayer mat in my fist.

'What's a gheebah?' she beams, blinking away the moisture from her eyelashes and nodding at me like now I am the two-year-old.

Is it worth educating her about gheebah? My hands smooth over the corners of my prayer mat, my fingers twisting the strands at the edges. Vanessa smiles again, showing me her disgusting teeth.

'It's Bengali for lunch.'

MELANIN

Ayusha Nand

DEITIES

When I was in Delhi, I was watching a South Asian news channel on a flatscreen television and an ad had come on. I was like nine. My mum and grandmother were in the kitchen making pani puri and the cool herbaceous smell was filling up the house. The sacred banners and deities were just chilling on the wall. The ad was about a dark-skinned girl who applied to be a receptionist and her dad was like, 'You will never be a receptionist because you're dark. If you're dark you won't get anywhere in life.' The dark-skinned girl was really upset so she went out to get this cream which was called Fair and Lovely. This cream is very popular and when I was younger, I used to use it because the media told me if you are fair you are pretty. Anyways, back to the ad. The dark-skinned girl used the cream, became fair-skinned, and her parents accepted her. She got the job and got married. I also used this cream because my family and South Asian culture influenced me to become fair. But now that I've grown, I'm happy having the amount of melanin that I have. This is still by far the shittiest ad I've ever seen.

SAY ESHAY

Blonde hair, light coloured eyes, generally lighter skin, freckles and flip-flops. I don't feel Australian because I don't fit the stereotypical Australian look. I don't use the slang they use apart from eshay. I say eshay a lot but that's really it. I also don't like flip-flops, they hurt my toes.

VIOLETTA

Pamela Asare

I put cocoa butter on her skin until it
glistened like melted chocolate on a sun-soaked day;
her small plastic body in my little arms,
wrapped in a pink crocheted blankie
that I got from Anglicare for a dollar fifty,
right opposite Auntie Amma's hair salon.

I wished my Baby Born had hair.
It would be kinky-curly like mine
and I would tie it up in small afro puffs
the way my mum used to do for me.

I cried the day my brother Kofi
threw her down the stairs.
A goal scored.
His cola face beaming above
his lanky frame.

Violetta, my Violetta.
Round shiny ebony face,
honey-tinted brown eyes.
I loved that she looked like me.

I remember begging my mum
to get me a Black Baby Born for Christmas.
And she did, along with a pink cot.
I told all my friends at Greenway Public.
I knew they were jealous because
they listened too much and did not butt in.

I used to feed Violetta with fake fufu and soup.
My mum said I was wasting all the flour.
I didn't care, I would just do it in secret.

When my mum became bloated with more than just food,
she said I would be getting a little sister.
I didn't ask for that!

But when I saw Yaaya's hair,
with her curls shining like black gold,
and when I heard her cry, she was mine.

When Yaaya's hair grew long enough,
I tied it up in small afro puffs
with rainbow-coloured hair ties.

My little sister always cried
but I did it for her anyway.
Afterwards, I would cuddle her
and she would laugh
in soft squeaking sounds
that did not take
a hand to squeeze.

I gave Violetta to my little sister.
She played with her just once.

Then I found Violetta
with her round ebony face dusty,
lying naked in a wardrobe.

I guess my little sister didn't need
a Black Baby Born like I did
because my Yaaya, my sweet Yaaya,
she had me.

THE DEVIL'S DRINK

Natalia Figueroa Barroso

LA LEYENDA DEL KA'A YARÎI

From the stick comes the splinter,
Yarîi feels the drumming on her chest.
From the seed form the roots,
her hasyva father she must help rest.

To the ka'aguy they find shelter
under acacias, jacarandas and azaras.
There, Yarîi learns to be supple
like a puma wandering through the selva.

When her father burns with fever,
Yarîi seeks for yuyos in the forest,
foraging through leaves, barks and sticks.

When their py'a rumbles for food,
she hunts like a kuimba'e and gathers like the kuña
before her, wiping dried saliva
off her parched lips.

Like a manganga piercing skin,
guilt inflames her father's insides.

To God Tupá he confides,
'Bendice a mi Yarîi.
Liberala de esta vida abrazadera,
su sabor salado,
su peso de hierro.'

Jasy the moon, Arai the cloud, adore from above.
Streams of light flood,
          cleansing
                              quenching
                                                  fertilising
the land, the river of colourful birds –
Uruguái.

A visitor wrapped in a soft brown gown
is camouflaged by the tree trunks.
His long white beard glows
as he walks out of the night
and into the campfire's light;
his protruding clavicles reaching out for food,
like a newborn searching for their mother's teat.

Despite her own exhaustion,
Yarîi receives the visitor
as the leaves absorb sunrays;
engulfing her days and
cutting her time,
making her father fill up with mud and
heavy rock on his tongue.

But Yarîi offers Tambú,
worm of white meat.
Raised in troncos of palmera pindó,

waiting for the exact hour
when los gusanos mature and are delicious to eat.

A wind separates Arai away from Jasy.
Moonlight beams upon the visitor,
revealing Tupá, the supreme God of all creation.

Tupá speaks,
'Yarîi debajo de esta tierra fértil,
un ka'a, Yarîi crecerá de tu mano.
No temas de sus verdes y blancos,
o su olor amargo.
Preparalo en agua hirviendo.
Cebalo en tu mate.
Fuerte siempre seras,
como la guerrera que sos.
Rodeada siempre estarás,
como la jungla con sus bichos.'

MATEADAS CON LA CHULA

The air smells of freshly boiled water,
humid and warm to the nostril.
The steam touches my ear.
Green bitter yerba sings to me
like the tamboriles to the vedette.
Chula knocks on our shared-wall
and screams like a steaming caldera,
'¡Empezó la telenovela!'
          Knock
                    knock
                              knock.

'¡El mate esta pronto!'
Like a cachorro greeting its owner,
I race to Chula's front yard.
Old television set balancing on
the windowsill.

Juan holding the antenna,
pacing back and forth
as everyone yells,
'¡Ahí! – There!'
I love joining the circle of vecinos
that el mate lured in.

Each family has its own serving rituals
but there's some rules we can all agree with:
'Don't touch my bombilla or I'll slap your hand',
a 'gracias' means 'no more', and
bubbles floating over leaves means we're la reina o el rey.

Chula ceba the first mate and
clockwise it goes.
Round after round,
        hold
                drink
                        slurp.

There's always one germaphobe
who doesn't want to drink till the end
because, 'I heard fulana sucks all the mates in town.'

But Chula always puts them in penitencia
with her slapping words,
'¿Mijo, you scared of my baba?
¡Chupa, this boca is cleaner
than your toilet, muchacho!'

That slurp though, it's the best.
It's like letting go of the week's work
with one noisy suck.

Chula rotates the yerba with her bombilla.
'¡Gurises vengan,
que el mate esta un poco lavado!'
The call the kids have been waiting for.
It's time for their serve of drink.
The mate is now a little washed,
not as strong in flavour, less bitter.
Perfect for the gurises – the kids.
'Cuidado,' Chula warns the children.
'Everyone has a burnt story,
so treat the mate with respect and it'll share
the entire barrio's gossip.'

SALSIPUEDES

Often, I dream of those off-white sails
flapping in the wind.

Our river of colourful birds
calling
alerting
warning.

The muddy sand hindering
those wooden vessels,
carrying sickly pale men within.

Over three hundred years of turmoil.

Then General Rivera meets with Venado, our Charrúa chief,
to speak of peace.
Instead he spikes the mate.
Hold
drink
slurp.

Venado's tongue becomes heavy and dry.
A smoke he craves
but his hands are numb.

Deceitfully, General Rivera offers to cut his tobacco.
Innocently, Venado offers his knife.
Instead, he cuts him into pieces and
throws him into the arroyo.
His blood awakens the selva,
the message is loud: 'Sal si puedes – Leave if you can.'

It feels like the acid's being extracted
from my stomach
as I imagine what came next.

With shotguns that flashed fuego.
With germs that ended days.
Men that spread legs with force.
Chains that rubbed to raw bone.

Maggot infested wounds.
Orders and new rules.
Enslaving women and children.
Killing men on sight.

Baptising White guilt
with new gods that devilled our drink
because our mate burnt their tongue.

BEIT SAMRA

Sara Saleh

The afternoon the militia showed up on Beit Samra's doorstep, the four El Husseini women were in a frenzy of fried food, mops and broomsticks and clouds of glistening powder that guaranteed a younger appearance. Although Jamilah did not know it then, the romantic version of Beit Samra that she had grown up with, the Beit Samra that had grown her, was about to end.

The turned-up tip of Jamilah's nose wrinkled at the aroma of bharat that padded the air. In the El Husseini family, food was an apology, a party, a funeral. Tonight, it was a katb kteb, the official Islamic ceremony where the mazoon came to officiate Saad and Amal's union. This was to be followed by a small celebration between the two families, crowned by a chorus of zaghrutas from Layla, her duty as the oldest sister. Presently, the whole event would not go for longer than an hour, the El Husseini girls had been confined to cooking and cleaning duties for the last week with Mama at the helm.

Popping her head into the lounge, Jamilah found it had been reshuffled once again – the centre table that was usually aligned beneath the crystal chandelier moved to the side to make room for smaller tables assembled into each other like crates. They were covered with white porcelain ashtrays and small clear glass bowls filled with salted pistachios, raw almonds and roasted honey cashews. There were vases of white and green flowers on either side of the room, an antique mahogany cabinet in one corner and an electric fan, which they plugged in when they had electricity, in the other. Maroon runners lined with gold sequins and a polished metallic pewter centrepiece overflowing with rosary beads draped the centre table. White plates were stacked on one end alongside a golden tray of ribbon-rimmed glass flutes, the special glassware that Mama had been stockpiling in a locked cabinet over the years. Boxes of assorted baklava and cellophane – wrapped plates of biscuits sprinkled with pistachio and powdered sugar and decorated with almond slivers and maraschino cherries in the middle – had been laid out.

Poor Baba... Mama probably had him out on errands all night, Jamilah thought. She knew he would spend the rest of the day hiding in the shop downstairs, claiming to work until maghrib when the Al-Masis were due to arrive. Jamilah also suspected Mama was glad to have him out of her way. This was her ship to steer.

As she trudged into the kitchen, Jamilah could make out Mama's low hum of words. 'You are not to make yourself too available,' she asserted. 'Be coy but confident, feminine but firm. This is what a respectable lady does.'

'You can hide out in the bathroom. Or pretend to be asleep!' Layla eagerly threw her suggestions at Amal. 'And if he tries to wake you up, run out crying. The poor man won't know what to do.'

'You are too much,' Amal laughed hysterically.

'Saba7 el khair.' Jamilah cleared her throat and pretended to adjust the straps of her dress.

Amal and Layla were on the kitchen table spooning a mixture of white cheese and specks of parsley into flattened palm-sized circles of dough. They folded the circles to create half-moon shapes, gently pinching the edges and indenting little lines in with a fork. There were two more slabs of smooth dough still untouched.

'Finally you have graced us,' Amal snapped, burrowing her long perfectly pencilled-in eyebrows across her forehead. 'We have so much left to do.'

Inheriting Mama's short-curvy stature, soft-milky skin and full-rosy cheeks, Amal's dainty features were hard to ignore. Her lids were always painted with shimmery plum shades because it accentuated the hazel specks in her light brown eyes. Behind her back, Layla and Jamilah referred to her as Fairouz, after the iconic singer. Amal was a diva but without the talent that earned her the right to behave like one.

People could tell Layla and Amal were sisters. Though taller and more statuesque, Layla was an exaggerated version of Amal, all the best qualities stretched in the worst ways; each feature sharper, deeper and rounder, mismatched on her face.

'Your daughters are all pretty, smalla, but hand on heart, none compare to Amal.' This was how the hairdressers at Tala's Beauty Salon fawned whenever the girls went and how every visiting auntie started conversations with Mama before they enquired about Amal's status.

Mama gave a short polite laugh laced with haughtiness as she declined. 'Amal is our eldest and you know how fathers can be. He is waiting to find someone worthy of her.'

Hunched over the stove, dyed dark brown coiffed curls swept behind a white silk headband, Mama was stirring a large wooden spoon through mincemeat sprinkled with pine nuts. There was a jumbo-sized half-covered pot with rivulets of smoke spiralling out of it.

'I am almost done with the mixture, you can get started on the meat ones in a minute,' Mama signalled to Layla and Amal. Turning to Jamilah, she said, 'I need you to run to Faddoul's. He promised me the most delicious freshly roasted cardamom coffee beans in all of Beit Samra today. Our guests will be most pleased.'

Nodding, Jamilah was relieved that Mama, with little faith in her domestic abilities, had assigned her a task that involved being out of the house.

'Now, I won't remind you all...' Mama began. The kitchen was her pulpit and her daughters her unwilling disciples. 'I don't want to hear or see a single thing out of line tonight.' She gestured a warning with her hands. 'The Al-Masis are a good match for us. They will look after Amal.'

Although Mama was petite, she always filled up the space she was in. She was heavily perfumed in her signature jasmine scent and dressed perfectly even when they had nowhere to go. She turned to Amal, whose eyebrows were now arched like two bird wings. She was hanging on to Mama's every word.

'They are also... aware of our situation,' Mama said. 'It does not affect them in the slightest nor is it their concern. But if they ask, I will know how to respond. You are to keep your mouths shut.' Like a skilled marksman, Mama always had her aim sharp and focused on one thing: securing the good fortune of each and every one of her daughters.

Amal believed Mama had it right with her lifelong mantra of 'a husband and a house'. This was a path to being seen and being safe – to surviving a society that hated them as Palestinians and as women. Saad was from a wealthy Saudi Arabian merchant family that had established the centre of their small perfumery empire in Beirut, the commerce and fashion hub of the region before the war broke out. Saad would provide for and take care of her. She did not want to end up like Aunt Suzanne, who died a spinster soon after her parents passed, probably from being old and alone. Or like Tamara, her school friend's sister who was thirty-two, still unmarried and the town's cautionary tale. 'A strange one she is,' Mama's friends reported. 'All that freedom has gotten to her head.' And she especially didn't want to continue life as a noncitizen, a nonperson. Living with no papers in Lebanon was like having a fever that never went away. It meant no medicine for Baba's diabetes (did they want to risk the cheap counterfeits?), no high school for them (unless they could afford the astronomical tuition at some fancy private French-run institution), no state university education in certain courses (Layla couldn't be a pharmacist like she had dreamed), and no job security and stable income since the government had banned Palestinians from almost all professions. To Amal, the stigma was punishment enough. It meant living cautiously, not trusting their friends or neighbours and not letting them into their lives – not really. Amal didn't want to let a piece of paper control her and her decisions. She wasn't sure she wanted a man to do that either but at least marriage was security, an antidote to the affliction of perennial uncertainty. Amal would play the lead role of Saad's wife, which came with citizenship rights once the curtains were drawn that evening.

Just as Mama had taught her, Amal had every word and every interaction planned to the last detail. She was to wear a fitted white abaya trimmed with exquisite gold lace embroidery along the sleeves and the frays of the belt cinched at her waist. She had it tailored to her exact liking. Her and Mama spent a month back and forth from the seamstress in nearby Burj Al Barajneh. Amal was not thrilled at first. She preferred to go to one of the prestigious dressmakers in Hamra in downtown Beirut – Saad could afford it. Hamra, or as the Francophones at school called it, the Champs-Élysées of Beirut, was brimming with fashion stores, theatres, restaurants, coffee shops and famous boutique hotels. Scholars and philosophers visited it, artists and poets wrote about it. Hamra had every trinket imaginable. Amal wanted to furnish her home and fill her wardrobe and fuss over what bonbonnière to have at the wedding. But Mama did not want to risk it. The checkpoints and clashes in different pockets of the city made her very nervous, especially after her brother Abdelqader's death three years before. But Beit Samra was safe from all that. Nobody cared for the unassuming town in the rugged and twisting Khalde mountainside overlooking the soft sparkling waters of the Mediterranean coast.

—

On her way back home from Faddoul's, buoyed by the sweet aroma of cardamom flaring in her nostrils, Jamilah spotted groups of armed men in dark clothes marching up to the mouth of Beit Samra. They were casually carrying combat gear, AK-47s and small launchers like loaves of flatbread. Although they were too far away to catch sight of her, she ducked behind a rusty white truck parked on the side of the road. Her mind raced as she clutched the bag of coffee beans tight to her chest, her eyes darting to locate the quickest escape route. As she snuck through Beit Samra's familiar knots, she pictured Abu Ali rolling his watermelon cart through the neighbourhood, echoes of 'bateeeekh' spreading through the town like hymns every single summer night. She remembered the Nazly al-Hoss School for Children with Special Needs, the first in the whole Khalde area. And how its namesake, the Prime Minister's wife, had attended the opening not too long ago as video cameras and journalists trailed behind her. Jamila thought of Faddoul, who to this day sold them bonjus for five liras even though the price had inflated to twelve because of the war. How he handed out steaming salty cheese and sesame ka'aks on Fridays to the men who spent the afternoon disguising political exchanges as noon prayers at the Othman Ibn Affan Mosque. Starved men always had a way of making things unholy.

As she turned the corner onto their street, Jamilah realised the raspy rapid heaving breathing disrupting the eerie stillness was coming from her. She held her breath as she laid eyes on her family's two-storey buttery yellow building. 'Ya rab! Ya rab!'

The building was standing in small pools of shrapnel that crushed the jasmine bushes in the driveway. A cloud of dust had moved in from down the block, the school abruptly the site of commotion Jamilah couldn't quite make out. The glass at Baba's garage-turned-paint-shop next door had cracked.

Imagining the worst, Jamilah dashed up to the house, her vision blurry. She could see nothing else but the thirty-six steps, the same steps Baba came up at the end of each day as he proclaimed, 'Assalum ayalkom'. They had not installed an elevator like they were supposed to – this was pointless because electricity was out except for Tuesday and Thursday and Saturday evenings. Oh how the generator they shared with the paint shop groaned and coughed whenever the family flicked on their small electric fans!

Jamilah reached the top step and jumped through the brown oak door, which had been left wide open.

'The wedding is off...' Amal was a scramble of words, whimpers and sobs. Her pale face scrunched up like paper as Mama and Layla comforted her.

'Alhamdullilah! You're okay!' Baba grabbed Jamilah by the shoulders. 'The school was hit. We don't know what's going on or why.'

Mama and Amal had been in the kitchen mixing olive oil with lemon juice for the tabbouleh when large pieces of debris flung into the kitchen balcony just missing them.

'We've been trying to get in touch with the Al-Masis but it's been ringing out,' he said. 'The news is reporting that militia are spreading across Beirut and the outskirts. They are also circling in on the camps. This might have been an accident or...' he paused. 'They might be getting ready to attack.'

An hour later, the kitchen radio blared with breaking news that answered their questions. Christian militia and Israeli soldiers were on a rampage. They had now entered the camps in West Beirut and were slaughtering Palestinian refugees and Lebanese Shias. The El Huessinis recoiled in horror as they listened to what was happening less than twenty kilometres away from them. Their faces turned all shades as the news reported grenades being tossed into houses, rifles spraying whole families and butchers' knives carving into their victims. Israeli army tanks had sealed off the camps and there was no escape.

'We need to go,' Mama muttered, her curls undone and plastered to her face with tear stains splotching her cheeks. 'The minute it's safe, we need to go.'

For five days and nights, the El Husseinis watched as bombs hung from the sky like fluorescent light bulbs. Layla and Amal retreated to their rooms, barely eating the rationed tin cans of chicken spam and fava beans that were quickly running out from the pantry and sleeping even less. They had not yet heard from the Al-Masis. Baba stopped going to work. Instead, he paced the hallway back and forth for hours on end. He never switched off the radio, even when it descended to static. He was waiting for the fighting to pause. It escalated and the killing continued. The Israeli army had invaded Lebanon with the intention of hunting down every last Palestinian and anyone else who got in their way. Rescuers and medics spent days digging through the wreckage of the bombed buildings, searching for trapped survivors. They mostly found bloodbaths and bones ground into dust.

Jamilah, who, much like her family, considered herself a Ramadan and Eid Muslim, observed every prayer from dawn until dusk. She implored God to protect them, to stop the shelling before it rearranged the shape of their country like a tawla board. She felt helpless seeing Mama drift aimlessly around the house. Mama's shoulders sagged with sadness. When she did speak, she sighed and groaned, lamenting the betrayal to their people and their humanity. All this against the sound of firing bullets, blood splatter and children choking on their own organs in Sabra and Shatila. The wedding preparations felt like a lifetime ago. How long until the men came for them?

On the sixth day, a God-given window of escape opened up. Baba rushed into the girls' room. 'They're saying an American family of four was killed in an ambush. The fighting will cease for a day or two. Now is our chance.'

At 2am, under the cover of a starless liquid night, the El Husseinis squeezed into their pale blue Ford, along with three garbage bags of clothes, bottles of water and their unspeakable grief. The Ford was tiny and tight, octopus limbs poking out everywhere. Baba wanted to avoid the different checkpoints. Some targeting Muslims, others targeting Christians, and many targeting both. Israeli fighter jets had also been targeting bridges and roads in the south western suburbs of Beirut. The El Husseinis weaved their way through the cobbled lanes, crooked alleyways and dirt paths that ran across the country like chaotic crisscrossed cables. Jamilah looked straight ahead, reciting a quick prayer and releasing an exhale that had lodged itself like a bone in her throat.

MICRO AGGRESSIVE FICTION

THE WHITE DON'T LIKE THE BLACK

Nellie Tapu Nonumalo Mu

In my first time in Australia at school, student laugh at me because my skin is black and my bag a big hole on it. And I start crying because the White don't like the Black people. So now the White people look at me and I feel unhappy.

TRUMP IS AUSSIE

Cassandra Taylor

spray tan
wrinkles
blond hair
massive suit
i don't know

CHINA IS EVERYWHERE

Noor Abuzamaq

Last two months, I am scared. All the world scared from the Coronavirus. Coronavirus it started in China but now is not just in China is everywhere. Is now in Australia also the place we live in it. First, I didn't care about the Virus but now there are many people have this Virus and I am really scared because I am coming to school every day and I meet a lot of people. I hope the Government should close the schools and we have to stay home a few days.

NOT RACIST?

Dezheen Shivan

My mum she had dark brown hair. She had dark brown eyes. She had light brown skin. I cried and shouted, 'Mum! Where are you?' She was very sad. I told to her, 'Next time you hold my hand.'

WALK AWAY

Fiti Fainifo

Next day, I was walking to the street and there was a boy standing in there and I walk there and stand there with him and he walk away. The number of my bus is 880. The boy has white skin and black eye.

SHE WHITE SKIN

Elisha Toese

Last week on Thursday, I was so surprise because my teacher said fa'afafine and her name is Winnie. She came from Tongan. When she said fa'afafine, I was so surprise because I thought she can't speak like that but she did! I thought she can't because she's not look like Tongan, she white skin.

HIGH SPEED

Mahran Asghari

In the car on my birthday. 60KMPH on the dash. Zooming past the Bankstown shops. My mum takes a peek at her phone while turning a tight corner: ssssskkkkkkkkkkrrrrrrrrrrrr! An Asian man in his fifties rocking slides and a walking stick pops out of nowhere. My mum shouts in a scrouchy voice: 'You had no right to walk there! I will call the cops on you. Go back to your country!' *Wait. Are we not Asians too?*

MEDIUM WHITE

Lara Ahmed

My first day at this school, I met Noor. She has a medium white skin and a brown eyes. She wears hijab. At the beginning, it was really weird, specially that it's my first school here in Australia. Anyways, Noor helped me to know the direction of the school. She's really nice and lovely. At the first day, a fight happened between two boys and Noor was so close to be hitten by them. Today, it's my fourth day at the school and I already feel that I've been here since ages. I'm really having fun and that's it. Noor wants to be an Egyptian ra2asa when she grow up.

AUNTY MOE

Sopanha Chea

A silent road in front of my house. Doing my math homework in my rainbow light room. The piggycorn sitting on my wood desk was looking at me. Family members were sleeping on the pink and black couch in front of the big flat TV. After a while, there was the sound of a woman screaming in Chinese. I hurried to tell everyone. 'Should we call the cops?' I asked my sister. She didn't reply, just went back to sleep. With my anxious mind made up and my body covered in sweat, I ran through our back gate toward the screaming woman's house. I quietly sat in the bushes on the left side of her fence, listening, watching. I saw a White man with a blue T-shirt, blue jeans, blond hair, honey beard. His strong body was standing in the woman's living room. I saw her wearing a red dress with her black hair and her slim body sitting on the gold couch crying. She was a kind and friendly neighbour – her name was Aunty Moe. She just moved in about half a year ago. I don't know what happened to her family but I know that she was living alone in that big house.

POLITZIER

Yash Bab

THROW SMOKE

My suburb is very unclean.
Smoke smells like a truck running.
People throw smoke in markets like a banana peel.

DOG WITH A PEANUT

When I saw my adopted brother, he looked like a dog with a peanut on his head. He looked like 🥫. We adopted him because he was a little 👶. When we picked him up, he started to 😃 like a kloun.

AUSSIE AUSSIE AUSSIE OI OI OI

Zoyal Dahal

AND NOTHING

A yellow-skinned thirteen-year-old female with big brown eyes and dark brown hair plus who is short. That's what I am and nothing like tall, white, blonde, freckled, flip-flop-wearing Australians.

MOST AUSTRALIANS

An Australian to me is a pale White person with blue eyes, pure blonde hair and freckles everywhere. Some can be the druggies in the West of Sydney while others rich with their $25 avocado toast on a fancy café near the beach in the North of Sydney. They use slang like arvo, bloody, sh$t, barbie, youse and g'day. Their Christmases are hot and they celebrate the queen's birthday in the cold. They are very tall and wear tank tops with flip-flops showing their yucky stubby toes with yellow long crooked nails and their VERY pale feet with a sock line like no other where one side is WHITE while the other is tan. I imagine most Australians on the outback riding kangaroos that turn them tanner. Idk but yeah.

UNFINISHED UNTANNED

Cleveland Brown

Donald Trump you yellow hair'd son of a bitch! You unfinished untanned butt cheek. You wanking cock sucker go fuck yourself we're getting a new president who's not racist like you ya spastic fuck.

PROXIMITY TO BLAKNESS

Max Edwards

The idea that being in a relationship with or having a connection to an Aboriginal person somehow absolves White people of racism is a myth. It is a myth that is a consistent response from those who have been called out on their racism. Their desire to prove a lack of racism by demonstrating proximity to Blakness through relationships such as family, friends and current or previous partners, dehumanises us. Like the small business owner who, in response to my question about whether an 'Aboriginal print' for sale was in fact created by an Aboriginal artist, said, unprompted, that she had an Indigenous step-daughter. As if our existence was evidence enough that she should be absolved of any cultural appropriation and harm. The desire to prove a lack of racism conceives us as nothing more than props, only acknowledged when we can be of use and of benefit as a shield against claims of racism or micro-aggressions.

Humans are complex beings and so too are the relationships that form between us. It is entirely possible to love and care for someone but have your ignorance harm them. It reminds me of a friend of mine who I have known for decades. Once, she proudly shared her experience hiking a mountain that is a sacred men's area with no thought to the cultural violation she had committed or my growing concern for her spiritual wellbeing having committed such a violation. Oftentimes, we get to choose relationships and whether to continue in them. Choosing to continue relationships with those who hold harmful (i.e. White supremacist) values towards us means we take on the burden of educating the other person. We do this whilst trying to avoid the harsh blows that come with someone we care about engaging in daily racism towards us. Such as the cherished friend of many years who casually asked me who 'discovered' the river we had just passed by, as if our diverse cultures and peoples weren't already in existence here for millennia. Or the much-loved relative who, upon being told I was travelling to Darwin, laughed and said I was going to where the 'real Blackfellas' were (because obviously being born in Warrang/Sydney meant I was 'a pretend Blackfella'). In these instances, emotional vulnerability becomes a liability. This dynamic means we may never really get to fully exist in, take comfort in, or experience, the fullness of those relationships unimpacted by racism.

The impact of racism is felt but the much-needed language to identify and label the racism has not yet been developed, so challenging racism 'in the moment' may not be a possibility. In some ways, it is easier to deal with the outright racists of the world as they are often ridiculed or readily identified for their extreme views and unapologetic White supremacy. It's the nice acquaintance who compliments our outfit in one sentence and then enquires about the 'free home loans' we get in the next. It's tiring challenging that kind of covert racism. Therefore, it's often less traumatic to keep the peace and let statements go unchallenged in order to maintain our own sanity and wellbeing. There are occasions where our physical safety depends on it. The violent and wrongful arrest of an innocent Aboriginal teenager, who was thrown into a fence, capsicum sprayed and handcuffed despite police searching for someone twice his age, is a case in point. The racism is blatant but challenging it in the moment isn't an option, in fact labelling the racism in circumstances like these is guaranteed to result in further violence.

When colonial power structures are added and imbued with White supremacist ideals and values, as is the case with all settler colonial societies, racism inevitably infects those people we love and hold dear. It is the system they are raised in and taught to uphold from birth. It is a system that privileges them, and so like those before them, they invest and uphold that system because they cannot conceive of anything different. To maintain their comfort, they deny themselves the opportunity for spiritual and personal growth and the possibility to heal from the traumatic colonial legacy they've inherited. Until and unless, of course, they are educated by us to view the world in a different manner. bell hooks tells us that 'love is an action, a participatory emotion'. It is a labour of love to invest in educating someone to learn and unlearn the racism they have internalised over their lifetime, all the while never being sure our efforts will pay off.

Proximity and access to us means those in a relationship with us have work to do. Their 'work' must ensure they act in ways that maintain our cultural safety at all times. Originally conceived by Māori nurses, 'cultural safety' is often understood as an environment which is spiritually, socially and emotionally safe, as well as physically safe for us; where there is no assault, challenge or denial of our identity, of who we are and what we need. The challenge is getting from theory to practice. Relationships are fundamentally experiential and human beings are multifaceted; only those who share the connection can truly know what cultural safety looks and feels like for them. Clearly though, as a minimum, it must include a conscious effort to let go of the idea that proximity and access to us equates to a lack of racism. In my mind, cultural safety is the lifelong commitment to unlearn the harmful messages and values about our peoples. It is a commitment to loudly and explicitly advocate for our right to exist free from the violence of the State and the full respect and recognition of our rights to our respective Countries, languages and cultures. It is moving from passive ally to accomplice. All of these actions undertaken consistently have the potential to embed cultural safety within the relationships between Aboriginal and non-Aboriginal peoples.

There are rarely absolutes in life when it comes to people. It's taken time, but I have cultivated my personal relationships so that those who bring love and joy into my life are well aware of the injustices we face as a people and act to limit that injustice where they can. There are also people in my life who have chosen to carry the burden of education. Such as the time my best friend, who upon hearing work colleagues question someone's Aboriginality because of his fair skin, interrupted and informed them that Aboriginal people have varying skin tones. I trust that their love and care for me will eventually be put into practice by challenging racism and White supremacy in all its manifestations – including within their own selves. Only time will tell.

CONCLUSION

Sarah Ayoub

I only cried once in the four years it took to complete my PhD. It wasn't because I was struggling with the subject matter, or the workload, or the COVID-19 pandemic that shifted the deadline. It wasn't because I fell pregnant twice during my candidature, which culminated in me caring for three children before my submission date. No, the only time I cried was when an acquaintance of mine invalidated my topic.

We were sitting by a playground in a Western Sydney park while our respective children played around us when she asked me how my thesis was going. 'It's been confronting,' I admitted. 'It's opened my eyes to the fact that books I loved as a kid were racist.'

She laughed dismissively, waving a well-manicured hand in my face. 'Really?' she asked. 'I find it hard to believe that racism still exists in Australia today.'

I looked at her, perplexed. 'Are you serious?' I responded. 'We can start with the fact that over four hundred Indigenous people have died in custody since 1991, or the fact that as recently as 2019, an Australian White supremacist slaughtered fifty-one Muslims praying in their mosque in New Zealand, or the fact that people with Asian or Middle Eastern surnames are more likely to have their resumes knocked back than those with Anglo surnames.'

'But—' she tried to interrupt.

'Or just the simple fact that Australians feel comfortable hurling racial slurs at footy games and on public transport...'

She shook her head at me, frustrated. 'But do you really think it's that big of an issue?' she pressed, giving me a condescending smile that still irks me to this day. 'I have white skin and I get racist remarks walking around Liverpool if I'm in a skirt because Arab men think I'm White.'

'That's not racism, that's sexism,' I pointed out.

Our conversation eventually got to the point where I was berated for wanting to write 100,000 words on something that was less worthy a cause – according to her – than poverty in developing nations or the persecution of Christians in parts of Africa and the Arab world. I was crushed, but I managed to politely bid her farewell before bundling my children into the car, tears flowing.

What a flake, I can imagine you thinking, *crying because someone disagreed with you*. However, my tears weren't about the argument but rather the uncomfortable realisation that despite our settler colonial origins to the politicians elected on xenophobic platforms to everything in between, people in Australia still believed racism wasn't real, nor relevant a discussion point.

In recent years, racism has played a game of subterfuge and won. It ingrained itself in attitudes that labelled 'Change the Date' activists as bandwagoners; in conversations that began with 'Wow, your

English is really good' to a fourth-generation Chinese-Australian born in Albury; and in social media posts arguing, in the wake of George Floyd's death and the subsequent amplification of Black Lives Matter protests, that 'All Lives Matter'. It rendered anti-racists as people who couldn't take a joke, and it defended comedians like Chris Lilley (who built his fame on performing brownface, blackface and yellowface), as an 'incredible talent... so observant of human nature'.

The fact that many Australians see Lilley's minstrel and outdated portrayal of a marginalised community as 'observant of human nature' only demonstrates that we have become desensitised to racism. After all, racism greets us every morning on the news: March 2018, Channel Seven's *Sunrise* ran a segment featuring an all-White panel that discussed Aboriginal adoption, calling the placement of Aboriginal kids in White families 'a no brainer'. Commentator Prue MacSween – who has no experience in Indigenous affairs or child welfare – opined that the Stolen Generation was justified and explicitly stated that we 'need' another one. The reaction was one of condemnation from Indigenous Australians and their allies, who protested outside the large glass windows that form the backdrop of the show in Sydney's Martin Place. Rather than address the criticism, *Sunrise* chose to conceal the protest by running previously-shot footage of Martin Place behind their presenters, closing the studio's soundproof blinds. This incident is the perfect metaphor for White Australia's inability to engage in racism: just pretend it's not happening.

We also see racism rear its ugly head in the evenings, as evidenced by the appearance of Sweatshop's Director, Dr Michael Mohammed Ahmad, on the ABC's *Q+A* program in 2018. When arguing that anyone who is a 'racist, White supremacist, colonialist, imperialist, orientalist, Islamophobe and xenophobe' should be afraid of him because he stands in solidarity with people who oppose bigotry and hatred, Ahmad was pressed by host Tony Jones to clarify that he meant they ought to fear his 'pen or typewriter'. Offering Ahmad the 'opportunity' to reassure Australians that he is not violent is a prime example of the stereotype and essentialism that greets Arab and Muslim males on a daily basis – you are presumed to be a threat until proven otherwise.

Failing to address such bigotry is not coincidental; it is an attempt at gaslighting and dismissing people of colour in a way that invalidates our experiences. As this book went to print, a student of African background at Adelaide's Trinity College had circulated a petition urging the school to take allegations of racism seriously, after it was revealed that students from the school posted a video of themselves lynching a Black doll from a tree to social media. The school responded by saying that there were 'racist elements' in the students' actions but denied they were racially motivated. Trinity College reportedly accused the student who started the petition of 'bullying' for calling on the faculty to address racism 'instead of excusing the incident as a learning curve'. That White Australia will generally respond to bigotry by sweeping it under the rug is one thing, but to deliberately silence accusations of racism rather than acknowledge a fault and seek to remedy it is another. And yet, these examples only scratch the surface, demonstrating that racism is indeed a regular part of the Australian story.

In fact, one could argue, racism *is* the Australian story. After all, early Australian literature actually made a case for White supremacy. From initial colonial days and well into the 1930s, First Nations people were depicted as savages and cannibals, and literature for children and adults extolled the virtues of colonisation and White superiority. In the late 1950s, migrants disembarking on Australian soil were handed free copies of Nino Culotta's *They're a Weird Mob*, which was written under pseudonym by an Anglo-Australian man named John

O'Grady. The book, which was later turned into a film, asserted the merits of assimilation, professing that 'there is no better way of life than that of the [White] Australian'. And in 1990, Michael and Rhonda Grey's *The Stew that Grew* was released. According to Arab-Australian anthropologist Ghassan Hage, this children's book functioned as an allegory for Australian multiculturalism in its depiction of migrants from a host of ethnicities each contributing an ingredient to a dish termed 'Eureka Stew'. The book, Hage argues, celebrates a 'White nation fantasy' in which White Australians imagine themselves as the 'managers' and 'masters' of the cultural diversity of their nation. The White Australian character, Blue, is in control of cooking the stew, and the 'ethnics' are depicted as suffering from exhaustion and hunger at the margins, seemingly devoid of agency, until they are invited to participate in the process of making the stew. The fact that this book was written for children is a prime example of the way that White supremacy operates in Australia. Many of us are subjected to it from childhood thanks to a curriculum which, until recently, celebrated Captain Cook's supposed 'discovery' of this land.

More than thirty years after *The Stew that Grew* was published, the hierarchy of 'us' and 'them' is still prevalent in Australia: people of colour are often granted a place in Australian society on the condition that they flavour the stew based on whatever White Australia deems appropriate. 'Obey the law in Australia or ship out of Australia.' These were the words of then-NSW Premier Bob Carr back in 2003, reminding us that if we weren't White, we were never truly seen as Australians, no matter what our birth certificates said.

Many Australians from minorities grow up believing – as it was iterated in events like Harmony Day and song lyrics like 'I am, you are, we are Australian' – that the country we live in is inclusive, and that everyone is seen equally, treated justly and welcomed accordingly. But our lived experiences are often very different, and having our identities demonised by government and media alike results in questions of identity, place and belonging that continue to affect us well into our adulthood.

This collection of stories is the embodiment of our experiences, reflections and questions. Comprehensive, hard-hitting and honest, *Racism: Stories on Fear, Hate & Bigotry* invites and challenges our fellow citizens to sit in our experiences, no matter how confronting they might be, in order to shift the Australian narrative from one of denial and distancing to one of genuine understanding and love.

As the writers in this book have demonstrated, racism takes many forms. It is both systemic and social. It doesn't have to involve physical violence on public transport for it to hurt. It doesn't have to manifest itself in a way that can be prosecuted. And it doesn't have to take the form of a hate rally: five thousand White Australians on a beach chanting 'No Lebs' and physically assaulting anyone they can find who looks Middle Eastern. To draw from Dr Martin Luther King Jr.'s 1963 'I Have a Dream' speech, racism can be as subtle as judging a person by the colour of their skin instead of the content of their character.

In *Black Looks: Race and Representation*, scholar, activist and critic, bell hooks, states that 'the issue of race and representation is not just a question of critiquing the status quo', but a matter of 'transforming the image' – to question and subvert existing narratives, consider alternatives and 'transform our worldviews'. Like other titles in the Sweatshop catalogue, *Racism: Stories on Fear, Hate & Bigotry* is an anthology that transforms the images and ideas we have about what racism is, what it looks and sounds like, and how it feels.

In offering Indigenous writers and writers of colour a space to share their stories, this book is a step towards transformation. These stories are no longer chips on our shoulders or scars on our skin or evidence of the storms we have weathered for daring to deviate from the norm. These stories are weapons in literature's shift towards change. They are no longer committed to memory but to print: re-writing our past, challenging our present, and remedying our future.

MORE FROM SWEATSHOP

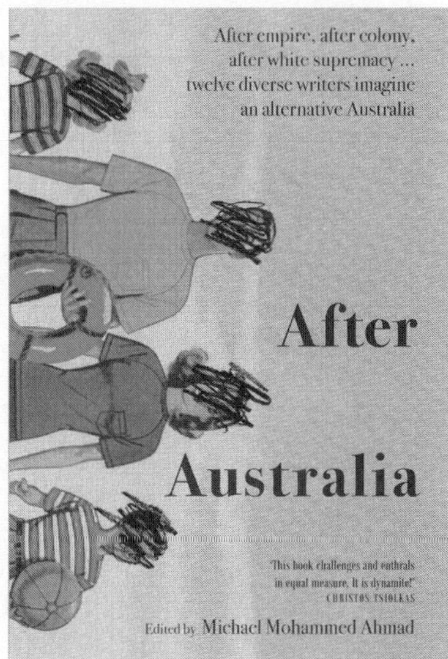

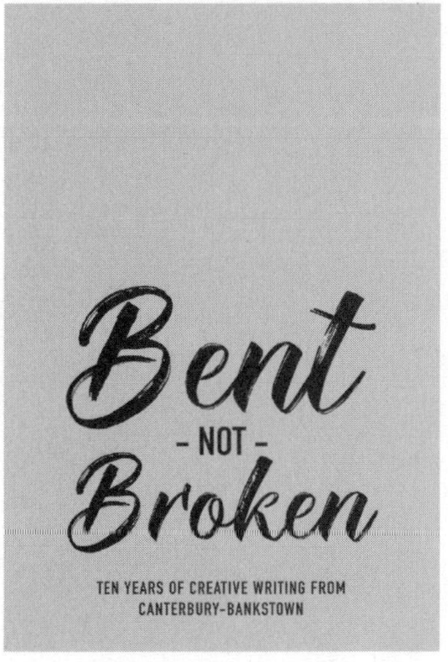

WWW.SWEATSHOP.WS

MORE FROM SWEATSHOP

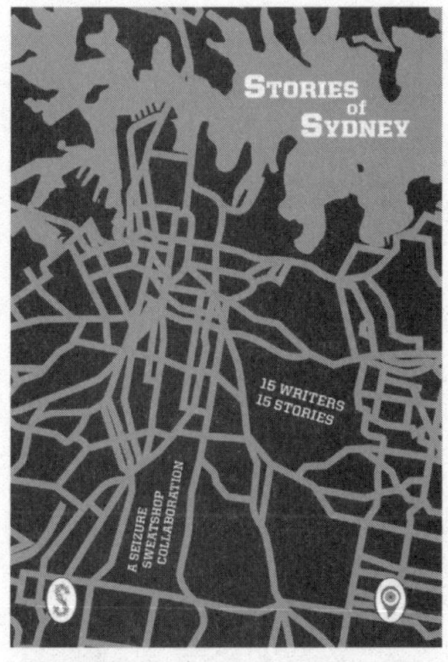

WWW.SWEATSHOP.WS